USING AND GROWING TREES IN YOUR GARDEN

A complete guide to choosing, landscaping, planting, pruning and propagating

Practical advice, step-by-step techniques and over 400 stunning pictures

Mike Buffin

southwater

To Carla, Zoë and Joshua, for all their inspiration, help and support.

This edition is published by Southwater, an imprint of Anness Publishing Ltd, Hermes House, 88–89 Blackfriars Road, London SE1 8HA; tel. 020 7401 2077; fax 020 7633 9499

www.southwaterbooks.com; www.annesspublishing.com

If you like the images in this book and would like to investigate using them for publishing, promotions or advertising, please visit our website www.practicalpictures.com for more information.

UK agent: The Manning Partnership Ltd; tel. 01225 478444; fax 01225 478440; sales@manning-partnership.co.uk
UK distributor: Grantham Book Services Ltd; tel. 01476 541080; fax 01476 541061; orders@gbs.tbs-ltd.co.uk
North American agent/distributor: National Book Network; tel. 301 459 3366; fax 301 429 5746; www.nbnbooks.com
Australian agent/distributor: Pan Macmillan Australia; tel. 1300 135 113; fax 1300 135 103; customer.service@macmillan.com.au
New Zealand agent/distributor: David Bateman Ltd; tel. (09) 415 7664; fax (09) 415 8892

Publisher: Joanna Lorenz
Senior Managing Editor: Conor Kilgallon
Project Editors: Lucy Doncaster, Clare Hill and Elizabeth Woodland
Copy Editor: Lydia Darbyshire
Designer: Mike Morey
Cover Designer: Balley Design Associates
Production Controller: Don Campaniello

Acknowledgements
Unless listed below, photographs are © Anness Publishing Ltd
GARDEN WORLD IMAGES: 41 top (J. Need); 41 bottom (C. Hawes).

Ethical Trading Policy
Because of our ongoing ecological investment programme, you, as our customer, can have the pleasure and reassurance of knowing that a tree is being cultivated on your behalf to naturally replace the materials used to make the book you are holding. For further information about this scheme, go to www.annesspublishing.com/trees

Previously published as part of a larger volume, *The Gardener's Guide to Planting and Growing Trees*

Main cover image: *Acer palmatum* with a brilliant display of scarlet leaves; Page 1: *Prunus* 'Accolade'; Page 2: *Acer japonicum* 'Vitifolium'; Page 4, top middle: Betula *papyrifera*; bottom left: *Pyrus calleryana* 'Chanticleer'; bottom right: *Quercus rubra*; Page 5, top left: *Psidium guajava*; top right: *Stewartia pseudocamellia*; bottom middle: *Tecoma stans*.

Contents

The importance of trees

Trees are one of the most complex and successful forms of plant life on earth. They have been around for 370 million years.

With their myriad shades of green and stunning flowers, foliage, fruit and bark, trees make our gardens, countryside and urban areas more colourful and spiritually uplifting. They do also increase wildlife diversity, since trees provide a habitat for countless species, from birds to tiny invertebrates, many of which we may not notice, but which are important elements of the ecosystem. Trees also help to purify the air, and planting them can benefit the environment as well as making our gardens more beautiful.

This highly visual manual gives clear guidance on choosing trees to suit your garden design, and how to plant and care for them. Simple, step-by-step sequences show all the techniques you will need, including staking, pruning and propagating, as well as dealing with pests and diseases, to ensure that trees will be a constant source of delight in your garden.

Trees provide an ever-changing backdrop to our lives. Through the different seasons, they provide a beauty that is breathtaking.

What are trees?

Trees are one of the oldest living forms of plant life. They also live longer than any other organism on the planet. In California, USA, there are Bristlecone pines that are known to be over 4,500 years old and in the UK there are yew trees of similar age.

Colonization by trees

Trees are amazing organisms that have evolved over millennia to colonize a wide and diverse range of habitats around the world. They inhabit many natural and urban landscapes, and have adapted to survive in almost any circumstances. This astonishing diversity can be seen in the range of trees that grow in our gardens.

Trees cover almost a third of the earth's dry land and there are estimated to be more than 80,000 different species, ranging from small Arctic willows that are only a few inches high, to the lofty giant coast redwoods, which can grow to an amazing 113m (368ft).

The role of trees

Trees have always played an integral part in human development by providing food, shelter, shade, medicines, timber and fuel, among other things. They also serve to feed and shelter all kinds of wildlife and increase its diversity.

This beautiful *Nyssa sylvatica* (tupelo), like all trees, plays a vital role in the ecology of the earth.

What defines a tree is an open question. The laburnum on the right is always classified as a tree, while the virburnum on the left is designated a shrub, but here they both serve as trees.

Forests of trees help to regulate water flow and can reduce the effects of flooding and soil erosion. They also influence weather patterns by increasing humidity and generating rainfall. But more than that, trees are essential to animal life – they process vast amounts of carbon dioxide from the atmosphere by absorbing it through their leaves and then emit life-giving oxygen, which we breathe in.

However, despite their wonderful benefits, humans are putting the future of trees at risk. Over ten per cent of the world's trees are now endangered. More than 8,750 species are threatened with extinction – and some are literally down to their last one or two specimens.

Longevity

Trees are very long lived compared to shrubs or other plants. The longevity of different types of tree varies tremendously; a short-lived tree like a cherry tree may last between 50 and 100 years, while a long-lived tree such as an oak may live between 100 and 700 years – or even longer.

Definition of a tree

For most purposes, a tree may be defined as a large, woody plant with a trunk that persists above ground all year. The main feaure distinguishing it from a shrub is that the trunk, clear of branches, is normally a significant proportion of the total height of the tree. Trees also differ from shrubs in that they have secondary branches that are supported on the single main stem or trunk.

Some definitions give a minimum size for a mature specimen, but heights and spreads vary widely and there are many exceptions to any rule on this – a large shrub can be much bigger than a small tree.

Tree or shrub?

Distinguishing between a tree and a shrub might seem a straightforward task, but the differences between the two are often subtle. We expect a tree to be tall, with branches and leaves held high above a clear trunk, while a shrub is supposed to be smaller, with a multitude of branches originating from close to the ground. However, as with most things in nature, plants can be difficult to categorize and sometimes a tree can be grown as a shrub – and vice versa. This is due to climate, altitude, exposure, soil, rainfall, shade, health and vigour – as well as interventional pruning to deliberately make a tree a shrub, or a shrub a tree.

The mighty coast redwood (*Sequoia semperivens*) can live up to 2,000 years, and is the tallest tree in the world, reaching up to 113m (368ft) in height and 7m (23ft) in diameter at the base.

Because of the great diversity of their habitats, some tree families contain massive specimens, while closely related species can be much smaller, resembling shrubs in both their growth and habit, but which are still called trees.

Definition of a shrub

A shrub (or bush) is usually described as being smaller than a tree, but the main feature is that the 'trunk' forms only a small proportion of the overall height, and above the point where it branches there is no longer a central, vertical trunk that is significantly thicker than the other branches.

Many shrubs have several branches originating from, or close to, soil level. Although some shrubs can achieve tree-like proportions, there are few that produce a clear trunk.

Fruit and berries are often brightly coloured, since this attracts birds, which play an integral role in seed dispersal.

Like trees, shrubs produce a framework of branches. Many types are small and low-growing, whereas the only way that trees can be kept to these proportions is through regular pruning or bonsai.

Whether grown as a tree or to shrub-like proportions, *Acer palmatum* 'Osakazuki' will brighten up any garden, particularly during the autumn when its leaves turn a rich, vibrant red.

Sometimes there is a choice; you can grow a particular plant as either a tree or a shrub. Some maples, for example, can be small or large, depending on how they are trained, pruned and planted. When potted up in containers, their root development is restrained, and this limits the tree's ultimate height. This versatility means that anyone can potentially grow a tree – whether in the biggest garden or on the smallest patio.

In the face of such diversity, it is easy to understand why trees hold so many 'world records', such as the oldest, tallest and widest specimens, as shown in the box on the opposite page.

Tree facts

• The oldest living tree is the ancient bristlecone pine (*Pinus longaeva*), which is thought to be 4,733 years old. Bristlecone pines grow very slowly due to the extreme conditions found in the White Mountains, near the Sierra Nevada, California, USA, where they grow in the remains of what was once an ancient forest some 3,000m (10,000ft) above sea level. At this altitude the trees are battered by wind and rain and baked by the drying sun, conditions that have 'pruned' them into strange shapes and forced them to slow down their growth.
• The world's tallest living tree is the Stratosphere Giant, a coast redwood (*Sequoia sempervirens*), which was 112.6m (369ft) tall in 2002 when it was last measured. It was discovered in 2000, growing in the Rockefeller Forest at the Humboldt Redwoods State Park, California, USA.
• The tallest tree ever measured was an Australian eucalyptus (*Eucalyptus regnans*), which was found to be a staggering 132.6m (435ft) tall when measured in 1872, although other reports estimate that it may have measured over 150m (500ft). The Dyerville Giant, another coast redwood, was estimated to be 1,600 years old when it fell over in 1991. It measured 113.4m (372ft) in height, excluding the 1.5m (5ft) of buried trunk. Like many other monumental redwoods, it grew in Humboldt Redwoods State Park.
• The biggest living tree is the famous General Sherman, a wellingtonia (*Sequoiadendron giganteum*) growing in the Sequoia National Park in the Sierra Nevada, California. It is the largest living tree by volume in the world. The volume was estimated in 1975 and calculated to be approximately 1,486.6m^3 (52.5 cubic feet).
• The heaviest-ever tree record belongs to another coast redwood, which blew over in 1905 and had a total trunk volume of 2,549m^3 (90,000 cubic feet) and a mass of 3,300 tonnes (3,248 tons).
• The widest-spreading tree is the great banyan (*Ficus benghalensis*) growing in the Indian Botanical Garden in Calcutta, India. It covers a vast 1.2ha (3 acres). Its branches are supported by 1,775 stilt or supporting roots. This massive tree has a circumference of 412m (1,350ft) and was planted in 1787.

The widest-spreading tree in the world is a *Ficus benghalensis* (banyan).

• The earliest surviving species of tree that is still grown in gardens today is the maidenhair tree (*Ginkgo biloba*) of Zhejiang, China, which first appeared 160 million years ago during the Jurassic era, when it colonized several continents.
• Some types of ornamental cherry trees can live between 50 and 100 years, whereas a long-lived tree, such as a *Quercus* (oak), may live between 100 and 700 years – or even more.
• Britain is thought to have the largest population of 'ancient' trees compared with the rest of Europe.
• Some trees produce life-saving medicines. For example, Taxol (a drug used to treat cancer patients) can be produced from yew leaves, and aspirin was originally created from research into white willow bark, which is a natural source of salicin and other salicylates – compounds similar in structure to aspirin.
• Broad-leaved trees change colour in the autumn because the green chlorophyll in the leaf breaks down and is reabsorbed by the tree prior to leaf shed.
• Trees have adapted numerous methods to pollinate their flowers. Pollination can be as simple as wind dispersal, or pollination by insects or even bats.

Ginkgo biloba (maidenhair tree) is the earliest surviving species of tree still grown today.

The benefits of trees

Trees add immense beauty to our gardens: their fruit, foliage and flowers offer a dazzling array of colours and textures, while their forms soften the harsh lines of buildings and screen unsightly views. However, their value is practical as well as aesthetic.

Cleaning the air

Trees play a vital role in the environment, releasing oxygen into the atmosphere through the process of photosynthesis, as well as cleaning our air by filtering out pollutants. In addition to this, they can be used to provide security, privacy and shade in our gardens.

Air pollution is usually worse in towns and cities than in rural areas. Fortunately for us, garden and street trees are able to absorb many of the pollutants from the atmosphere, and heavier pollutants and dust particles sometimes adhere to the surfaces of leaves rather than being breathed in by us, until they are washed away by rainwater and into the nearest drain.

Improving soil

Tree roots help to bind the soil together, preventing soil erosion, by keeping it stable while allowing rainwater to drain into the soil. As they decompose, fallen leaves are dragged into the soil by worms and other soil-dwelling organisms, further improving the structure and moisture-retaining capacity of the soil, which helps to minimize run-off, which, in turn, reduces flooding.

Shade and shelter

In hot climates, trees can be grown to shade houses from direct sunlight, which experts have estimated can reduce the cost of air-conditioning by as much as 30 per cent. Similarly, planting trees to provide shelter from cold prevailing winds can also help to reduce winter heating bills.

Trees make effective shelter belts by protecting areas from damaging wind streams. The most effective shelter planting is an even mixture

Microclimate

Trees affect a garden's microclimate by slowing air movements and increasing humidity. This occurs because water is constantly evaporating from the surface of leaves during the growing season. Trees can also lower temperatures produced from the heating effect of concrete and brick buildings by providing shade. This creates a more acceptable climate for other plants as well as for us.

Power stations constantly pollute the atmosphere, but if the surrounding countryside is planted with trees, they will help to filter out pollutants.

Trees support all kinds of life, from birds and insects to fungi and lichens.

Trees can provide a windbreak and muffle unpleasant sounds such as road traffic. They are also invaluable in absorbing pollution.

of deciduous and evergreen species. This slows down the wind, rather than deflecting it up and over the windbreak, which would force the deflected air back behind the windbreak in a more turbulent way.

Noise absorbers

Trees planted in dense blocks can be used to reduce the level of traffic noise by providing a barrier that deadens the sound. Conversely, trees can be quite noisy themselves. The quaking aspen (*Populus tremuloides*) is often planted so that the continual rustling of its leaves competes with and helps to block out unwanted background noise.

Wildlife benefits

A major benefit of trees is their value to wildlife. Whenever we plant a new tree we will attract birds, animals and insects into our garden. In addition, because trees create shade and shelter for other plants, our garden environment becomes much more diverse and is able to develop into a more sustainable habitat, where beneficial insects can flourish and help to retain a natural balance between pests and diseases and their natural predators and prey.

Trees are also the natural habitat of birds and a wide variety of wild animals, which use the trees as a permanent or temporary home, or as a convenient shelter from bad weather or predators.

Trees provide protection and shade for other plants and are the natural habitat of a wide variety of wildlife, including birds and insects, which assist with pollination and seed dispersal.

The naming of trees

Like all plant names, tree names adopt botanical Latin as a universal language to avoid confusion caused by the many common names given to individual plants.

Naming confusion

The North American tulip tree is universally known as *Liriodendron tulipifera*. However, in various countries it has an array of common names, such as tulip poplar, tulip tree, yellow wood and canary whitewood. Some of these common names are used for other trees as well. For example, *Magnolia* x *soulangeana* is sometimes known as tulip tree. For this reason, botanical Latin is used as the definitive name.

Plant names are based on the relationships between plants and other nearby relatives. For example, the genera *Magnolia* and *Liriodendron* (tulip tree) belong to the same family, Magnoliaceae (which also includes the genera *Manglietia* and *Michelia*), and they are distinguished by the arrangement of petals, anthers, ovaries and styles of the flowers. It is these shared traits that put them in the same family. Although their flowers look similar, the plants' leaves, bark, trunk, size and habit may be quite different. This means that, even though magnolias and tulip trees both belong to the Magnoliaceae family, they are distant cousins rather than direct relatives.

Liriodendron tulipifera – otherwise known as tulip poplar, tulip tree, yellow wood or canary whitewood.

Trees such as *Liriodendron chinense* (Chinese tulip tree) and *Liriodendron tulipifera* (tulip tree) are classified as being directly related because they both belong to the Magnoliaceae family and because they look similar. The only differences are their overall height and distribution; one being found in China and Vietnam and the other along the eastern seaboard of North America.

In addition to these species, there are numerous other plants in the Magnoliaceae family, and these are found in both temperate and tropical zones of the world.

Magnolia grandiflora 'Goliath' has a highly descriptive name – both the species and cultivar names suggest the flower's large size.

Families

Tree families are large, generalized groups, whose members have some similar traits, such as susceptibility to particular diseases. Some, however, contain only a single genus. The names of plant families can be easily distinguished as most end in 'aceae'. For example, Aceraceae, Fagaceae and Magnoliaceae are, respectively, the maple, beech and magnolia families.

Genera

Below the botanical rank of family is genus (plural: genera), and again this is a large grouping of plants but with a higher number of shared characteristics than the family.

Within the family Fagaceae are the genera *Castanea* (chestnut), *Castanopsis*, *Chrysolepis* (golden chestnut), *Fagus* (beech), *Lithocarpus* (tan oak), *Nothofagus* (southern beech) and *Quercus* (oak), even though beech trees look different from oak trees.

Species

The second part of a tree's botanical name designates the species (sp.). For example, *Quercus robur* (common oak), *Quercus palustris* (pin oak) and *Quercus bicolor* (swamp white oak) are different species of oak tree. They are distinguished by their different leaves, habits and flowers, but they all belong to the genus *Quercus*.

Although each species within a genus has a different specific name, the same species name can be used in different genera: for example, *Quercus alba* (white oak) and *Abies alba* (European silver fir).

Occasionally, two plants have similar traits but still appear different, and an additional name may be required. This often occurs in the wild to distinguish individual populations. For example, the widely planted Australian species *Eucalyptus pauciflora* (snow gum) is distinguished from *E. pauciflora* subsp. *niphophila* (alpine snow gum), which grows at a higher altitude, is much hardier and has slightly narrower leaves. Because of these differences, it is designated as a subspecies of the snow gum.

Two other such subdivisions also exist. They are form or forma (f.) and variety (var.), both of which occur naturally in wild populations.

The botanical name of the Northern red oak, *Quercus rubra*, indicates the red colour in the species name – '*rubra*' is the Latin for 'red'.

Hybrids

Many tree species that grow close together, both in their wild habitats and in towns and gardens, will breed with trees of a different species and create offspring that are intermediate between both parents. These hybrids, which are signified by a multiplication sign (x), are usually of the same genus but different species. For example, hybrids between the deciduous *Quercus cerris* (Turkey oak) and the evergreen *Quercus suber* (cork oak) were named *Quercus* x *hispanica* (lucombe oak). A number of different forms have arisen and these tend to have intermediate leaf shapes between both parents and are also semi-evergreen.

There are also a few unusual hybrids, called graft hybrids or chimaeras (or chimeras), which arise when the tissues of two plants fuse and grow together. The resulting plant exhibits the leaves and flowers of both parents. The most commonly grown graft chimaera is + *Laburnocytisus adamii*, which is a hybrid of *Laburnum anagyroides* (common laburnum) and *Chamaecytisus purpureus* (syn. *Cytisus purpureus*; purple broom). The + sign denotes that this is an intergeneric hybrid between two different genera.

Cultivars

Trees that have originated in gardens, nurseries and among plant breeders are termed cultivars or cultivated varieties. Their names are given after the species name and are distinguished by single quotation marks. For example, *Quercus rubra* 'Aurea' is a selection of the red oak with leaves that are butter yellow when they emerge in spring but fade slowly to light green. It is similar in all other respects to the type species, *Quercus rubra*.

A cultivar name can also occur when a tree has been hybridized and one, but not both, of the parents is known. In these cases no species name is used. *Malus* 'John Downie', for example, is a hybrid crab apple of unknown parentage.

Groups

In recent years various propagation methods have resulted in the production of a number of similar-looking plants that are not identical clones (as happens with cultivars). These are known as Cultivar Groups. In such cases the plant name includes the word Group, which can result in some unwieldy names – for example, *Acer palmatum* var. *dissectum* Dissectum Atropurpureum Group and *Magnolia campbellii* (Raffillii Group) 'Charles Raffill'.

The structure of trees

Trees truly are marvels of nature. They are woody, perennial plants that have clearly defined trunks, which hold the branches and leaves towards the light to gain sustenance. Each part of a tree's structure is designed to give the tree the best chance of growing and thriving.

Wood

As trees grow, they produce a large, woody framework of roots, trunk and branches, which enables them to survive and thrive in many different climates and soil types.

The wood consists of a series of compartments or layers that grow each year. As these compartments grow, the tree increases in girth and height. The trunk and other woody parts of a tree (the branches and large anchoring roots) are made up of a number of distinct zones.

The woody trunk provides the structural strength of the tree, while a tough, waterproof bark protects the delicate tissues that transport water and nutrients to the leaves and simple sugars to all parts of the tree. These sugars are the energy that feeds the tree, and they are produced in the leaves.

Bark

The material that grows on the outside of the branches and trunk is called bark. It is a corky layer of dead cells and it prevents the tree from becoming too hot or too cold, protects it from moisture and allows the cells inside to breathe. The bark also protects the tree from boring insects, fungi and bacteria.

Most bark is waterproof, so the trunk beneath will not rot, but bark has to be able to breathe. It does this by way of tiny openings, called lenticels. These are the dark oval marks you can see on the trunk.

Each year, as the trunk and branches increase in girth, the bark splits and regrows. The ways in which the bark does this gives each species its individual bark pattern.

Some bark splits and falls in small, angular flakes, as is seen on *Pinus* spp. (pine), while the bark of *Eucalyptus* falls in long strips, and *Betula* (birch) shreds in papery strips. This enables bark to be constantly replaced by fresh tissue. In the case of *Platanus* x *hispanica*, it enables the tree to survive in a heavily polluted atmosphere, since the contaminated layer of bark is regularly shed – thus earning the tree the name of London plane, as it is widely planted in that city's streets.

Some trees have light, smooth bark. The thin, whitish bark of *Betula pendula* (silver birch) stops the trunk

THE STRUCTURE OF A TREE

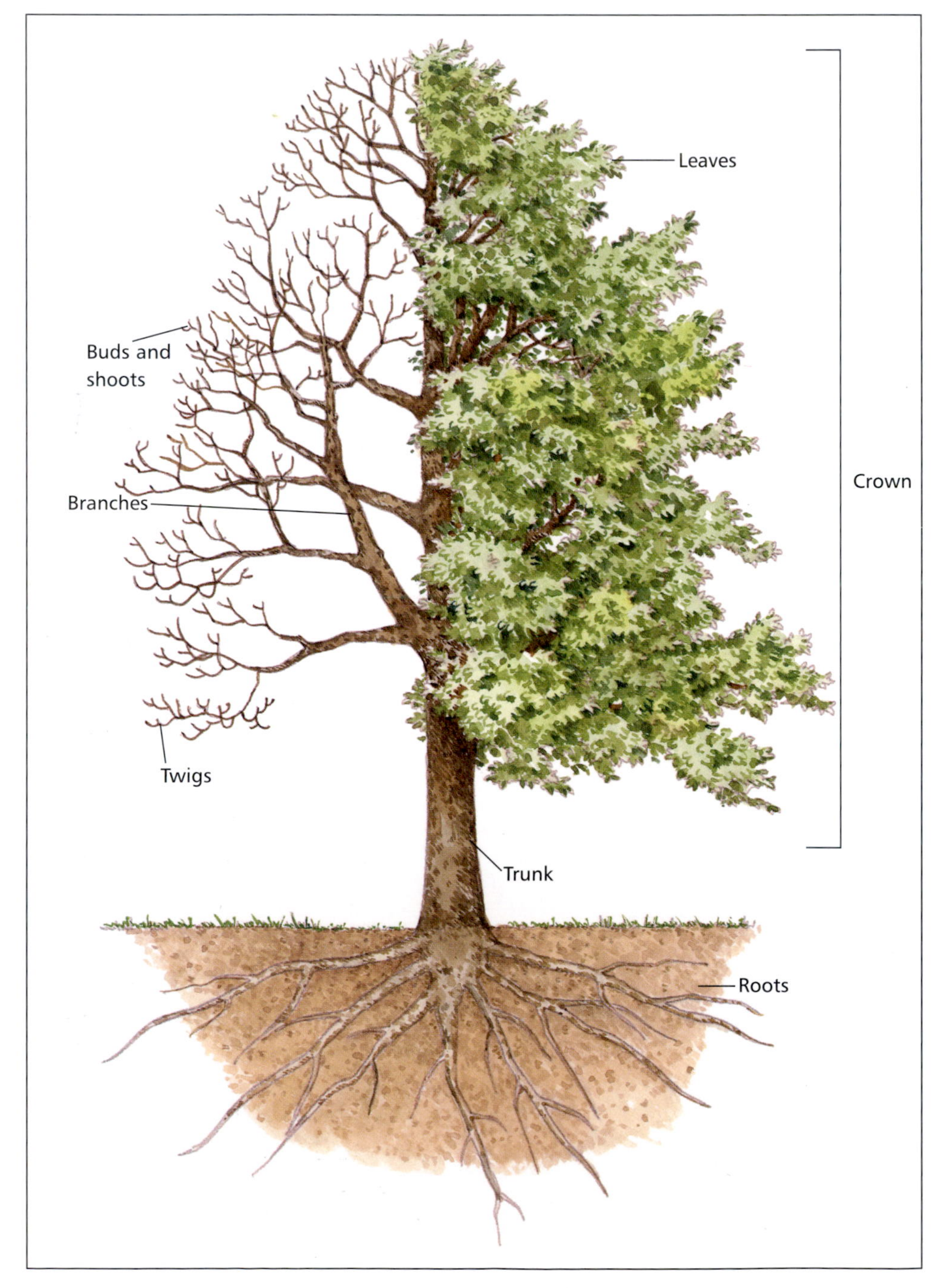

from overheating in summer and in winter, when reflection from lying snow can cause air temperatures to rise quickly and split frozen wood.

The trunks of many palm trees are covered with a matted layer of the fibrous remains of the leaf stalks, and this acts as insulation during hot weather. Some trees, such as the *Sequoiadendron giganteum* (Sierra redwood), have exceptionally thick bark, which is an adaptation that allows them to survive forest fires following lightning strikes.

Sapwood and heartwood

The sapwood consists of the outer annual growth rings in a tree's trunk, through which water and nutrients are carried from the roots upward to the branches, stems and leaves.

The heartwood is found at the centre of the trunk. It consists of old cells that have a high wood (lignin) content. This is a hardening material found in the cell walls of woody tissues and is the substance that gives trees their strength.

Although these cells are old, they are not dead; their growth has slowed, and they no longer breathe or require energy to continue to function. This heartwood acts like a skeleton, providing the framework on which the rest of the tree grows.

Calocedrus decurrens (incense cedar) has strongly corrugated bark.

The beauty of bark

Betula utilis var. *jacquemontii* 'Snow Queen'

Eucalyptus (gum tree)

Bark splits and regrows each year as the tree increases in girth. It may shred in shallow, paper-like sheets, in long strips, as on a eucalyptus, or in big flakes, as on some pine trees. The ways in which the bark splits and regrows give each species its individual bark pattern.

Many species are well known for their highly ornamental bark, including *Acer capillipes*, *A. davidii*, *A. grosseri* var. *hersii* and *A. pensylvanicum* (snakebark maples), *Betula* spp. (birch), *Eucalyptus* spp. (gum tree), *Prunus serrula* (Tibetan cherry), *Stewartia* spp., *Pinus* spp. (pine) and *Platanus* spp. (plane).

Some trees, such as *Acer griseum* (paperbark maple) and *Prunus serrula* (Tibetan cherry), have highly polished, mahogany-coloured bark, which shreds and hangs from the branches in winter. Any tree with shredding bark may be used as a focal point in the garden, and every effort should be made to position it so that it is backlit by the winter sun.

Trees with stark white bark, such as *Betula utilis* var. *jacquemontii* (Himalayan birch), can also be used to create a focal point in the garden, where the eerie, ghost-like stems will illuminate even the darkest of corners.

Cambium layer

Immediately beneath the bark and at the tips of roots and shoots is the cambium layer, which is the growth tissue of a tree. As it grows, the trunk, branches and the stems of a tree increase in size.

The cambium layer is made up of two types of living cell: phloem and xylem. The soft phloem cells transport nutrients and energy from the leaves to the rest of the plant and the woody (lignified) xylem cells transport water and support the tree.

The phloem and xylem cells divide and increase in number throughout the growing season, and this division process produces the annual rings we see in a tree trunk and which we use to age a tree when it is cut down.

In temperate climates the rings are produced from spring until autumn. However, in tropical climates, which have no distinct seasons, the rings are produced throughout the year. If the cambium layer is damaged sufficiently deeply to cut off the phloem and xylem cells, the tree cannot transport water and nutrients and may die.

Root system

Trees have an extensive root system that is made up of branch-like, woody structures designed to anchor the tree into the soil, while a network of much finer roots absorbs the nutrients and water. The farther they are away from the trunk, the finer roots become.

Growing from these fine roots are millions of tiny hairs, which absorb moisture and nutrients from the soil. These nutrients include minerals, which are essential for the tree's growth. The roots also store food, such as starch produced by the leaves, for later use.

The rings in a tree trunk are produced by the division of phloem and xylem cells.

Contrary to popular belief, most tree roots do not penetrate very deeply into the soil; the roots of even the tallest tree seldom reach down more than 3m (10ft). However, the roots spread quite wide just under the surface of the soil. As the top layers of the soil are usually rich in the organic material, minerals and moisture required to nourish the tree, they have no need to go much deeper, but every need to spread out.

How to date a tree

Some trees can live hundreds of years. Dating when they were planted is possible by reading the ring growth the tree produces. Each year the new cells that are produced under the bark create a new ring of tissue, visible in a cross section of the tree. The growth occurs at the outside of the trunk, just under the bark.

Each ring has light and dark sections. The light tissue is less dense and is made up of cells produced in the spring when the tree is growing at its fastest rate. The dark part of the ring is composed of cells laid down in the summer when the rate of growth has slowed. These rings are known as growth rings, with each light and dark ring pair representing a year of growth.

By counting the growth rings, it is possible to work out the age of the tree. The rings can be read either by taking a cross section of the trunk, if the tree is dead, or with just a core section taken from the trunk.

Root hairs have a lifespan of a few weeks and are constantly replaced.

Leaves

There are a huge number of different types of leaf, which come in a vast array of shapes, sizes, colours and textures. As well as being attractive, leaves play a vital role. They generate food so that the tree can live, grow and thrive. They do this using a process called photosynthesis, whereby the leaves absorb carbon dioxide and emit oxygen during the daytime.

Leaves contain a green pigment called chlorophyll that absorbs light energy from the sun. This energy is used to combine the carbon dioxide in the atmosphere with water taken up from the soil, creating glucose and oxygen.

The oxygen is released back into the atmosphere, but the glucose is used to provide energy and can be transformed into either starch or cellulose for storage or to form the cell walls of the tree.

Phloem cells in the cambium layer under the bark transport the sugary products of photosynthesis from the leaf to all other parts of the tree. This energy can either be stored for later use, used to produce flowers or seeds, or employed to heal any wounds the tree may receive.

Photosynthesis

The sugars that the tree uses to grow are produced by a process called photosynthesis, which involves nutrients, water, carbon dioxide and sunlight. Oxygen is a by-product of photosynthesis. The leaves of a tree are able to absorb and harness the power of sunlight, like a solar cell.

The cells that absorb sunlight (chloroplasts) are green and give the leaves their colour. All woody parts of a tree are able to store simple sugars, which the tree will use as an energy supply in winter or at times when growth is difficult, such as during a drought or an infestation of insects. Trees can also absorb carbon monoxide and help to filter and purify our environment.

Flowers

Considered by many to be the most delightful part, flowers herald a change in the seasons and reaffirm the cycle of life. Indeed, giving life is their function, as they are the reproductive part of the tree.

The range of flowers on trees is as remarkable as the different leaf forms. Most trees flower in spring or summer, although some temperate trees, such as *Parrotia persica* (Persian ironwood), reap the benefits of winter flowering. Many tropical trees bear decorative blooms throughout the year, as there is little change in conditions from season to season.

Flowers can vary in shape and size – from the cup-and-saucer pink and white flowers of *Magnolia campbellii*, which may be 30cm (12in) across, to the clusters of dainty flowers borne by spring-flowering cherries, such as *Prunus* 'Amanogawa' (ornamental cherry).

Most wind-pollinated trees evolved in areas where there was a shortage of insects, and so they are quite common in northern temperate zones of the world. Most conifers, for example, are wind pollinated.

Pollination by insects is much more common, however. Flowers that produce copious amounts of nectar attract insects, such as bees, but they need to get the attention of the insects first, and many trees are often highly scented for just this reason, with their aroma lingering for days.

Flowers of *Prunus sargentii* are a pretty shade of pink to attract pollinators.

Other trees bear flowers that open up to produce their intoxicating scent for only a day. Some trees flower at night so that their blooms may be pollinated by night-flying moths or bats.

DIFFERENT LEAF SHAPES

Metasequoia glyptostroboides (dawn redwood) has spirally arranged fern-like foliage (needles).

Liquidambar styraciflua 'Palo Alto' has maple-like (palmate) leaves that are alternate along the stem.

Carya ovata has leaves that are made up of five long, pointed leaflets. These are arranged along slender stems (rachis).

Male and female

Individual male sex cells are referred to as pollen. Individual female sex cells are contained in specialized cells, called ovules, which are normally located in flower parts. Fertilization is the name given to the fusing of pollen and ovule nuclei, leading to the formation of a seed.

Reproduction

Some trees, such as cherries, have male and female organs within the same flower and so can self-pollinate in order to reproduce. Others, such as hazels, have separate male and female flowers on the same tree.

Another group of trees only produce flowers of one sex, and therefore require another tree of the opposite sex to be somewhere in the vicinity in order to be pollinated.

Trees in the latter two groups cannot go out and search for a mate so they rely on a go-between to transport the pollen, either from the male to the female part of the tree or from a male tree to another tree of the opposite 'sex'. This can be achieved by wind, water or an animal.

This need to attract a vast array of potential pollinators has caused many trees to produce magnificent-looking and highly specialized flowers to act as a lure. Flowers that are pollinated by birds and butterflies tend to be tubular in shape in order to keep the nectar out of reach of other pollinators. As the birds bend in to collect the nectar, the pollen brushes on to them and is later transferred to another flower.

Seeds

Once the flowers have been pollinated, they develop into fruits of some kind, with the ultimate aim of dispersing seeds to begin a new generation of trees; each seed contains all that is necessary to start the creation of a new tree.

Dispersal occurs by different means. Some seeds, such as those of the maple, have 'wings' to aid dispersal by the wind. Nuts, for example, are buried by animals such as squirrels, which sometimes fail to return for them, thus leaving a 'planted seed'. Berries with small seeds are eaten by birds, which then excrete the seeds in their droppings. These fruits are usually brightly coloured, to attract birds, and contain nutritious flesh as well as the seeds.

Fruit

The production of fruit is often associated with autumn in temperate regions. This is because the warm weather of the growing season provides the best conditions for the development of fruits and seeds. In tropical countries, however, due to more favourable weather conditions fruit production can take place throughout the year.

The flowers of *Catalpa bignonioides* are trumpet-shaped. Pollinators collect the nectar and transfer pollen to other trees.

Conifers, such as *Juniperus chinensis* (Chinese juniper), bear their seeds in cones, which vary greatly in size and shape.

The seeds of the Seville orange (*Citrus aurantium*) are contained in the fleshy fruit.

Rowans produce brightly coloured berries that attract animals, which disperse the seeds.

Indian horse chestnut buds open to reveal down covered leaves.

Tree fruits range from the cones borne by coniferous species to drupes (stones enclosed in a soft, fleshy case), like mangoes and plums. There are also fleshy fruits such as oranges, small nuts, pea-like pods, spiky chestnuts, acorns and two-winged maple seeds. Many fruits are highly decorative and are a welcome addition when there is little else of interest in the garden.

The structure of seed

A seed consists of a protective shell and a food-storage facility that allows the germinating seed to start growing and, eventually, develop into a seedling. Inside every ripe tree seed are the beginnings of a root, shoot and one or two specialized leaves, known as cotyledons (palms are monocots). If a seed manages to be fertilized, it will either germinate immediately or wait until conditions are right for it to commence growth.

The first thing to emerge from the seed is the root. Whichever way the seed is lying, the root will instinctively grow downwards into the soil. Once established, the two cotyledons emerge and begin the process of photosynthesis. Shortly afterwards, true leaves appear from a bud between the cotyledons and the tree begins to grow.

Buds

A tree bud consists of next year's leaves, stems and often flowers, which are folded and twisted tightly together in a waterproof covering of modified leaves. These are known as bud scales. Sometimes extra protection is provided by a coating of hair, wax, resin or gum on the outside. Inside the bud is everything the tree will need to resume growing once the days lengthen and the temperature increases in spring.

As spring arrives, the buds begin to open and the leaves gradually emerge. Common factors such as warmth and light trigger off this process, but each species has its own particular triggers depending on its life cycle, which is affected by factors such as the length of the growing season in its geographical area.

Cones

Trees that bear their fruit in cones – usually brown, woody structures with scales – are called conifers. The reproductive organs are the male and female cones. The male cone produces the pollen, while the seed develops in the female cone, which is often larger in size.

The entire proces of reaching maturity, fertilization and seed ripening can take a number of years.

Cupressus abramsiana, like all conifers, bears its seeds in hard, protective cones.

Different types of tree

Trees fall into several distinctive categories, each of which has its own particular defining characteristics. These categories are: deciduous trees, evergreen trees, coniferous trees and palms. Each of these categories can be further divided into flowering trees and fruiting trees.

Deciduous trees

Trees that lose their leaves in autumn in response to lower light levels and falling temperatures are called deciduous trees. At this time of the year the green pigment in the leaves breaks down and the other coloured pigments in the leaves are revealed, producing a range of colours.

Even in tropical climates where the seasons are less defined and temperature and light levels are steady, the leaves of some trees turn attractive colours just before they fall. This is not, however, a response to low temperatures, but the result of the tree drawing back any useful minerals that remain in the leaf.

The leaves of the yellow birch, *Betula alleghaniensis*, turn yellow in autumn.

Quercus coccinea (scarlet oak) is a deciduous species native to North America.

Juglans ailanthifolia is a type of walnut, which is grown for its prized timber, spring catkins, autumn colour and fruits.

Popular deciduous trees

Acer spp. (maple)
Aesculus spp. (horse chestnut)
Alnus spp. (alder)
Betula spp. (birch)
Carpinus spp. (hornbeam)
Carya spp. (hickory)
Castanea spp. (sweet chestnut)
Catalpa bignonioides (bean trees)
Cornus (dogwood)
Corylus spp. (hazel)
Crataegus monogyna (common hawthorn)
Davidia (handkerchief tree, dove tree, ghost tree)
Diospyros virginiana (American persimmon, possumwood)
Fagus spp. (beech)
Fraxinus spp. (ash)
Ginkgo biloba (maidenhair fern)
Jacaranda mimosifolia (jacaranda)
Juglans spp. (walnut)
Koelreuteria spp. (gold pride of India)
Laburnum spp. (golden rain)
Larix spp. (larch)
Liquidambar spp. (sweetgum)
Liriodendron spp. (tulip tree)
Maackia spp.
Magnolia spp.
Malus spp. (crab apple)
M. domestica (common apple)
Metasequoia (dawn redwood)
Morus spp. (mulberry)
Nyssa spp. (blackgum)
Oxydendron (sorrel tree, sourwood)
Parrotia spp. (Persian ironwood)
Paulownia spp. (coffin tree)
Platanus spp. (plane)
Plumeria spp. (frangipani, temple tree, pagoda tree)
Populus spp. (poplar, aspen, cottonwood)
Prunus 'Accolade'
P. cerasifera (cherry plum, myrobalan)
P. 'Ichiyo'
P. sargentii (Sargent cherry)
P. 'Taihaku' (Great white cherry)
Pseudolarix amabilis (golden larch)
Pterocarya spp. (wing nut)
Punica granatum (pomegranate)
Pyrus spp. (pear)
Quercus spp. (oak)
Robinia spp. (acacia)
Salix spp. (willow, osier, sallow)
Sassasfras spp.
Sorbus (mountain ash/rowan)
Staphylea spp. (bladdernut)
Taxodium distichum (swamp cypress)
Tilia spp. (lime, linden)
Ulmus spp. (elm)
Zelkova spp.

Cryptomeria japonica 'Lobbii' is a beautiful cultivar of Japanese cedar.

Ficus benjamina, or weeping fig, has long, glossy dark green leaves and a weeping habit.

Popular evergreen trees

Acacia spp. (wattle)
Agathis spp.
Arbutus spp. (strawberry tree)
Banksia spp.
Calliandra spp. (powder puff tree)
Callistemon spp. (bottlebrush)
Calophyllum spp. (Alexandrian laurel)
Eucalyptus spp (gum tree)
Eucryphia spp.
Ficus spp. (fig)
Grevillea spp. (spider flower)
Ilex spp. (holly)
Lithocarpus spp. (tan oak)
Luma spp.
Magnolia delavayi
Magnolia grandiflora (Bull bay)
Maytenus spp. (mayten)
Michella (banana tree)
Metrosideros spp. (rata)
Pittosporum spp.
Protea spp.
Psidium spp. (guava)
Schefflera spp. (umbrella tree)
Tabebuia (trumpet tree)
Thuja spp. (arborvitae)
Tsuga spp. (hemlock)

Evergreen trees

Both tropical and temperate evergreen trees retain their leaves for longer than a year and then shed them gradually, so that they always have leaves. The advantage for the tree of retaining its leaves is that it has a longer growing period.

Some evergreen trees, such as some species of wattles, have very narrow leaves, which lose very little water during the hot summer months. In periods of extreme drought, however, they will lose all their leaves in order to conserve even more moisture.

Other species, such as *Magnolia grandiflora* (Bull bay), have glossy leaves that reflect sunlight and hairy undersides that help to reduce transpiration.

In tropical regions, most trees are evergreen because there is little to distinguish one season from the next, so the tree has less need to drop its leaves in one go. In cooler, temperate zones, where there is a marked difference between winter and summer temperatures and where freezing occurs, most evergreen trees are conifers, although some broadleaf evergreen trees can also be found. The term broadleaf distinguishes these trees from conifers, which have needle-like leaves. Broadleaf evergreen trees bear true flowers, rather than cones.

Arbutus unedo 'Elfin King' has a distinctively shaped strawberry-like fruit, which makes it a very popular evergreen tree for a small garden.

Conifers are extremely adaptable trees. Although many thrive in cold areas, they also have the ability to acclimatize themselves to a wide range of geographical areas and so are to be found in both temperate and tropical areas.

Coniferous trees

An ancient group of plants, there is fossil evidence for conifers reaching back over 300 million years. As a comparison, the first flowering plants began to evolve just 100 million years ago.

The world's tallest, largest, thickest and oldest plants are conifers. They are distinguished by the fact that they bear cones and their seeds are not protected by being encased in an ovary. Such trees are known as gymnosperms (naked seed).

Although conifers are found in a range of climates, they have adapted to grow in colder areas or high in mountains and hills where the ground is often covered by snow in winter. They produce a woody trunk with small radiating branches. Most have narrow leaves, which lose less moisture than broader leaves; this is important in winter when the soil is frozen, as well as in dry summers. Most are evergreens, retaining their needle-like leaves for longer than a year, sometimes for two or three years – sometimes for up to ten years. Some cone-bearing trees lose their leaves in winter to conserve energy, and these are known as deciduous conifers.

Abies bracteata, also known as Santa Lucia fir or bristlecone fir, is found in mountainous regions of Europe, North America, Asia and North Africa. Like most conifers it has needle-like leaves.

Popular conifers

Abies spp. (fir)
Agathis spp. (kauri palm, dammar pine)
Araucaria spp. (monkey puzzle)
Calocedrus spp. (incense cedar)
Cedrus spp. (cedar)
Cryptomeria japonica (Japanese cedar)
Cunninghamia spp. (Chinese fir)
Cupressus spp. (cypress)
Fitzroya cupressoides (Patagonian cypress)
Picea spp. (spruce)
Pinus spp. (pine)
Sciadopitys verticillata (Japanese umbrella pine)
Sequoia sempervirens (coast redwood, Californian redwood)
Sequoiadendron giganteum (sierra redwood, giant redwood, wellingtonia)
Taxus (yew)
Thuja spp. (arborvitae)
Thujopsis (hiba)
Tsuga spp. (hemlock)

Palm trees

Belonging to an ancient and distinct group of plants, palms are close relatives of bamboos, grasses and lilies. They are most prevalent in tropical and subtropical regions and only one other group of plants – orchids – exhibits greater diversity.

Some tropical palms have adapted to grow in swamps and in almost total shade, where they develop into massive plants in order to compete for the available light. They have even developed ways to climb up other trees. The greatest selection of palms comes from warm, humid climates, but there are a small number of hardier palms, widely grown in temperate climates, and a few island species are popular in coastal locations.

Palms are monocotyledons, which means that they have only one seed leaf, like grasses and bamboos. They have linear veined leaves and are not able to produce 'true' wood, as trees and shrubs do. The growth point of the palm is at the tip of the trunk, so if this dies, the whole palm will die.

Palms are adaptable landscape plants, which are included in gardens for their architectural foliage. They can provide height and texture, as well as being a framework for other bold foliage plants. A tall, established palm is a useful shade and upper-canopy tree. They also make excellent lawn specimens.

Palms range from compact forms, 1.8m (6ft) tall, to 30m (100ft) giants. Although they can be difficult to site in temperate landscapes, it is worth persevering because the bold, linear trunks and exotic palmate or fan-shaped foliage bring a tropical lushness to any garden, whatever the climate.

Roystonia (royal palm) has an upright form that is instantly recognizable against the skyline.

Palms tend to prefer hot climates, although some species – such as *Butia capitata* (pictured here), *Chamaerops humilis*, *Phoenix canariensis* and *Trachycarpus fortunei* – will do well in warm temperate areas, where winters are milder.

Popular palm trees

Bismarckia
Butia spp.
(yatay palm, jelly palm)
Caryota spp. (fishtail palm)
Chamaerops humilis
(dwarf fan palm, European fan palm)
Licuala spp. (palas)
Livistona spp. (fountain palm)
Phoenix spp. (date palm)
Roystonea spp. (royal palm)
Sabal spp. (palmetto)
Trachycarpus spp. (windmill palm)

Malus 'Red Jade' is named for the colour of its fruit, but the flowers are also highly decorative.

Bauhinia x *blakeana* produces highly fragrant, brightly coloured flowers.

Flowering trees

The vast majority of trees produce seeds that are encased in a protective shell or in a fruit, and these trees are termed angiosperms ('angio' being the Greek word for 'vessel'). This group of trees includes both deciduous and evergreen species that grow in both tropical and temperate climates.

Infinitely versatile, flowering trees have adapted to meet the challenges of a variety of different habitats by developing ingenious methods to pollinate their flowers. Some trees, like *Betula* spp. (birch), *Corylus* spp. (hazel), *Fagus* spp. (beech) and *Quercus* spp. (oak), are wind pollinated and, like conifers, bear insignificant flowers. Others have evolved to bear extremely decorative (and often scented) flowers, which attract insect pollinators.

Many fruit trees, including apples, pears, apricots, cherries and plums, as well as date and coconut palms, fall into this category, producing a wonderful display of stunning flowers every year.

Trees that are wind pollinated produce insignificant flowers. However, the ornamental cherries shown here rely on insects for cross-pollination and so produce fragrant, showy flowers.

Popular flowering trees

Aesculus spp. (horse chestnut/buckeye)
Albizia spp. (silk tree)
Aleurites spp. (candlenut)
Banksia spp. (banksia)
Brownea spp. (flame tree)
Calliandra spp. (powder puff tree)
Callistemon spp. (bottlebrush)
Cassia spp. (shower tree)
Catalpa spp. (bean tree)
Cercis spp. (Judas tree/redbud)
Citrus spp. (citrus)
Cladrastis spp. (yellow wood)
Cornus spp. (dogwood)
Crataegus spp. (hawthorns/haws)
Davidia involucrata (handkerchief tree)
Embothrium coccineum (Chilean fire bush)
Eucryphia spp.
Grevillea spp. (spider flower)
Halesia spp. (snowdrop tree)
Jacaranda spp. (jacaranda)
Koelreuteria spp. (golden rain tree)
Laburnum spp. (golden rain)
Lagerstroemia spp. (Crape myrtle)
Magnolia spp. and cvs. (magnolia)
Malus spp. and cvs. (crab apples)
Metrosideros spp. (rata)
Oxydendron arboreum (sorrel tree)
Paulownia spp. (empress tree)
Plumeria spp. (frangipani)
Portlandia grandiflora (tree lily)
Protea spp. (protea)
Prunus spp. and cvs (cherry)
Pyrus spp. and cvs (pear)
Tecoma spp. (yellow elder)

Citrus limon is a popular choice for growing under glass in a cool temperate climate.

Plum and cherry trees require moisture-retentive but free-draining soil.

Conference pears have a distinctive elongated shape, and are delicious raw or cooked.

Fruit trees

Both tropical and temperate fruit trees exist, and they may be deciduous or evergreen. Many species, such as *Malus domestica* (apple), have been hybridized for commercial reasons to produce forms bearing larger, tastier fruits, with improved disease resistance, and higher yield.

When choosing fruit trees for your garden, you must remember that, although some fruit trees are self-fertilizing and will produce a good crop on their own, most species will require a pollination partner, which must be a different variety of the same fruit species that flowers at about the same time and is compatible in other respects.

While temperate fruits, such as apples, peaches, pears and plums, can be grown relatively easily in tropical climates. Most tender tropical fruits are very difficult to grow in temperate climates unless they are given a lot of shelter or grown under glass. For many people, however, the rewards of producing exotic fruit make it worth the effort.

Crab apples, such as *Malus* 'Butterball', can be used as pollinators for domestic apples, and have the added benefit of being beautiful garden trees.

Popular fruit trees

Artocarpus altilis (breadfruit)
Carica papaya (papaya)
Citrus sinensis (sweet orange)
Eriobotrya japonica (loquat)
Litchi chinensis (lychee)
Malus domestica (apple)
Mangifera indica (mango)
Morus spp. (mulberry)
Olea europaea (olive)
Persea americana (avocado pear)
Prunus armeniaca (apricot)
P. avium (sweet cherry)
P. cerasus (sour cherry)
P. domestica (plum)
P. italica (greengage)
P. persica (peach)
Psidium guajava (common guava)
Punica granatum (pomegranate)
Pyrus communis (common pear)

Choosing trees for different climates

Trees are found all over the world except at the very highest altitudes and areas where the ground is frozen hard and covered by snow and ice all year round. The geographical extent of habitats in which trees can survive is a result of climatic conditions and they are classified according to their ability to thrive in certain areas.

Tropical trees

For obvious reasons, tropical trees are so called because they come from the tropics, a region of the world around the equator that is bounded by the Tropic of Cancer in the north and the Tropic of Capricorn in the southern hemisphere.

A tropical climate is classified as one that is warm and humid, and where the average temperature stays above 18°C (64°F) throughout the year. This means that in these regions the temperatures are relatively stable, and they are also frost-free. These regions do not have seasonal variations like those found in temperate zones.

Generally in the tropics the soils tend to be relatively poor, as a lot of the nutrients are washed out by the constant rain showers and downpours. However, tropical plants – many of which have beautiful flowers and foliage and are quite quick to grow and mature – can also be grown in subtropical zones, where temperatures may fall lower in the winter months than those of the tropics, but still remain frost-free.

In addition, climate change is increasing the range of tropical and subtropical trees that can be grown in temperate zones, where gardeners have always experimented with microclimates, with the result that the use of these trees is becoming more widespread.

Ailanthus altissima (tree of heaven) is very adaptable and will grow on poor soil.

The bottlebrush tree, *Callistemon citrinus* 'Splendens', is very drought-resistant, making it an ideal tree for subtropical, tropical and protected microclimates in warm temperate regions.

Tropical or temperate?

The tropics are defined as a geographic region, the centre of which is on the equator, and which is limited in latitude by the two tropics: the Tropic of Cancer in the northern hemisphere and the Tropic of Capricorn in the southern hemisphere. The tropics include all the parts of the Earth where the sun reaches an altitude of 90°, or a point directly overhead, at least once during the solar year.

In the temperate zones, which are north of the Tropic of Cancer and south of the Tropic of Capricorn, the sun never reaches an altitude of 90° or directly overhead.

A tropical climate is defined as a non-arid climate in which yearly mean temperatures are above 18°C (64°F). At latitudes higher and lower than subtropical, the climate is called temperate, with annual mean temperatures less than 20°C (68°F) and the warmest month achieving averages over 10°C (50°F).

Aesculus x *carnea* is a temperate tree that bears beautiful pink flowers in late spring.

Temperate *Cornus kousa* bears flowers in the summer and strawberry-like fruits in the autumn.

Acer saccharum (sugar maple) provides vivid autumn colour in temperate regions.

Temperate trees

Trees that can survive in a climate with four distinct seasons – spring, summer, autumn and winter – are known as temperate trees. In northerly latitudes winters are cold, with temperatures below freezing.

With such low temperatures, plants have had to adapt to survive; many trees lose all their leaves during the autumn and conserve energy by hibernating during winter (these are termed deciduous). Others retain their leaves to make the maximum use of the low light in winter; these include broad-leaved evergreens and most conifers.

Acacia dealbata (mimosa) is a subtropical evergreen tree that is frost-hardy.

In northern Europe, cold, long winters are the norm. Trees grown in this area need to be able to withstand low temperatures, while they await the arrival of spring.

Microclimate factors

The word microclimate is often used to refer to the prevailing conditions in a relatively small area, such as a woodland or forest, or even a garden.

Local effects

Microclimates are the conditions created by the effect of buildings, hedges and fences, as well as other trees and shrubs. The ways in which such factors affect the general climate in a geographical area sometimes allow us to grow plants that may not be naturally suited to the location.

Built-up areas often become what are known as 'urban heat islands', which is when a city or large town becomes warmer than the surrounding countryside. This phenomenon occurs because the hard surfaces of buildings and roads absorb heat during the day and release it at night and in the early morning, generating higher ambient temperatures in the vicinity.

Buildings can also slow down or divert winds, which can cause temperatures to rise. The heat generated by vehicles and given off from central-heating and air-conditioning systems also helps to increase the overall temperature in cities to a few degrees above that of the surrounding countryside.

A lack of trees and other vegetation in cities gives rise to far greater heat absorption than in less developed areas. In wooded areas, trees absorb heat during the day and, as they cool, their leaves release water vapour, which in turn cools the air. This process is called transpiration and it continues throughout the day as long as the trees have an adequate supply of water around their roots.

Walls that face the sun

On a small scale, we can create microclimates in our own gardens. For centuries, gardeners have used walls to protect tender plants. Walls that face the sun will absorb heat during the day and reflect it back into the surroundings in the evening. This extra warmth will allow wood to ripen sufficiently before the onset of winter, so that the tree behaves as if it is hardier than if it was grown in the open garden.

A tree-lined garden greatly reduces the movement of air within it, which allows for a higher relative humidity, as the air is loaded with evaporated water droplets produced through transpiration. Wind speeds also tend to be reduced by the filtering effect of the leaves and the various layers provided by shrubs and intermediate and top canopy trees.

Fences are often erected in gardens to screen a practical corner from view, or to provide support for a climber. In addition to these functions, fences will affect the microclimates in the garden by providing shelter from the wind and shade from the sun.

In a cool climate, the heat stored by a wall will improve the flowering and fruiting performance of a plum fan trained against it.

The temperature of the canopy of a dense forest will be different from the forest floor.

In tropical areas, a range of exotic trees and plants can flourish. Although cooler countries may covet such greenery, local microclimate factors make it impossible for these plants to thrive there.

Local temperature

The treetops of a high, dense forest can form an almost unbroken surface. During the day the treetops absorb sunlight, which results in high temperatures at the top of the canopy and lower temperatures below this level because of the natural shading effect of the trees.

Similarly, the garden floor is generally cooler than the canopy and surrounding countryside. The difference in daytime temperature in summer can be as much as 5°C (8–9°F). At night, the heat is trapped below the canopy so the air stays warmer longer.

Summer heat

It is now becoming widely recognized that summer temperatures are an important factor in a plant's survival, and a system of heat zones has been devised based on the number of days in a particular area when the temperature reaches at least 30°C (86°F). In much of North America the heat zones correspond to the hardiness zones, mainly because of geographical factors.

In North America, heat zones can be used to indicate areas where a plant might be at risk from prolonged high temperatures. In northern Europe, however, they can be used to indicate where a plant would not have sufficient warmth in summer to ripen the wood so that it could survive winter.

Most of the British Isles has a US hardiness zone rating of 8 or 9 but a heat zone rating of only 1 or 2. This is just one of the reasons why woody trees and palms that are widely grown and thrive in the southern states of the USA do not do well in Europe, unless they are grown in very protected and artificial environments, such as palm houses or conservatories.

As with all life, water is essential to a tree's survival. Climate change in recent years has meant that some trees are being adversely affected by drought and are therefore at risk.

Plant hardiness and zones

Hardiness is the word used to describe the type of climate in which a plant can survive. We often use the word as a shorthand way of describing a plant's ability to withstand cold temperatures; in the UK, plants are generally categorized as fully hardy, frost hardy, half-hardy, frost tender, and tender, depending on the minimum temperature they can tolerate, but it is more complicated than this. It also includes the plant's reactions to heat, cold, drought and wind, so understanding your microclimate will help you choose suitable trees for your garden. In Europe, the USA and Australia, hardiness zones are used to determine the suitability of plants for a particular area. However, hardiness zones are based solely on macroclimates, whereas the microclimate in a garden can be heavily influenced by local factors.

The US plant hardiness map divides North America into 11 hardiness zones. Zone 1 is the coldest; zone 11 is the warmest, and is a tropical area found only in Hawaii and southernmost Florida.

Yucca brevifolia (Joshua tree) thrives in arid desert conditions.

Pine trees, like many conifers, can withstand freezing temperatures.

In between the zones there is a predictable pattern across the continent, although a closer look will reveal scattered variations. Generally, however, the colder zones are found at higher latitudes and higher elevations.

The fact that plants commonly grown in the higher US zones do not flourish in the equivalent European zones suggests that there is more to plant hardiness than an ability to withstand low winter temperatures. Indeed, if minimum temperature was the only criterion, gardeners throughout northern Europe would be growing tender trees such as palms, oranges and olives outside.

These plants thrive in specialized microclimates and a wide range of factors other than winter cold will determine where a plant will grow successfully. It is, therefore, essential that you fully understand local growing conditions.

Other survival factors

Many other factors affect a plant's ability to succeed in a particular place. Individual plants may be affected by their provenance and breeding. The type of soil will affect whether a plant thrives as well as the availability of nutrients, the speed with which water drains and whether roots can penetrate to sufficient depth. Rainfall, in terms of both quantity and timing, is vital, and gardeners should also consider summer temperature, humidity and soil temperature. Finally, a plant may survive in a particular locality but may not flower if the day length is too short or too long or if it requires a period of low temperature in winter.

Stewartia pseudocamellia (Japanese stewartia) prefers moist, cool soils and light shade.

The large leaves of *Bismarckia nobilis* (noble palm) cast light shade.

Nyssa sinensis (Chinese tulepo) prefers to grow in heavy shade.

Plumeria alba (frangipani) casts heavy shade, due to its dense foliage.

Sun and shade

The light levels in a garden will affect your choice of tree because some species are more tolerant of shade than others.

The easiest way to decide if a tree is shade tolerant is to find out where it grows in the wild. The tree's ultimate size may also be an indication because small trees are often understorey species, in that they grow below taller trees, but like most things in nature there are always exceptions to the rule.

Trees that make good hedges are also usually shade tolerant, so if you have a shady garden you should look for species like *Carpinus betulus* (common hornbeam), *Chamaecyparis* spp. (false cypress), *Crataegus* spp. (hawthorn), x *Cupressocyparis leylandii* (Leyland cypress), *Fagus sylvatica* (common beech), *Taxus baccata* (common yew) and *Tsuga* spp. (hemlock).

The shade cast by trees is an important consideration in warmer climates, where summer shade is more desirable than it is in colder climates. Although palms cast dense shade due to their large leaves, the total shady area is less than a tree with a wider branch network.

Trees that cast light shade

- *Acacia* spp. (mimosa/wattles)
- *Acer buergerianum* (trident maple)
- *A. palmatum* (Japanese maple)
- *Betula* spp. (birch)
- *Bismarckia nobilis* (noble palm)
- *Brachychiton acerifolius* (flame tree)
- *Cassia* spp. (shower tree)
- *Cladrastis* spp. (yellow wood)
- *Eucryphia* spp.
- *Gleditsia* spp. (honey locust, Caspian locust)
- *Grevillea* spp. (spider flower)
- *Halesia* spp. (snowdrop tree)
- *Jacaranda mimosifolia*
- *Laburnum* spp. (golden rain)
- *Lagerstroemia* spp.
- *Livistona* spp. (fountain palm)
- *Maackia amurensis*
- *Nothofagus* spp. (southern beech)
- *Olea europea* (olive)
- *Protea exima*
- *Quercus alnifolia* (golden oak)
- *Rhamnus* spp. (buckthorn)
- *Robinia* spp. (locust, false acacia)
- *Roystonea* spp. (royal palm)
- *Sorbus aucuparia* (mountain ash)
- *Spathodea campanulata* (African tulip tree)
- *Stewartia* spp.
- *Styrax* spp. (snowbell tree)
- *Tabebuia* spp. (trumpet tree)
- *Trachycarpus* spp. (windmill palm)

Trees that cast heavy shade

- *Abies* spp. (fir)
- *Acer platanoides* (Norway maple)
- *A. pseudoplatanus* (sycamore)
- *Aesculus* spp. (horse chestnut/buckeye)
- *Arbutus* spp. (strawberry tree)
- *Artocarpus altilis* (breadfruit)
- *Brownea macrophylla* (Panama flame tree)
- *Castanea* spp. (sweet chestnut)
- *Cedrus* spp. (cedar)
- *Citrus* spp.
- *Dillenia indica* (chulta)
- *Eriobotrya japonica* (loquat)
- *Fagus* spp. (beech)
- *Ficus* spp. (fig)
- *Juglans* spp. (walnut)
- *Ligustrum lucidum* (Chinese privet)
- *Liquidambar* spp. (sweet gum)
- *Lithocarpus* spp. (tan oak)
- *Magnolia grandiflora* (bull bay magnolia)
- *Metrosideros* spp. (rata)
- *Pinus* spp. (pine)
- *Plumeria* spp. (frangipani)
- *Pterocarya* spp. (wing nut)
- *Quercus* spp. (oak)
- *Salix* spp. (willow)
- *Schefflera actinophylla* (umbrella tree)
- *Sequoia sempervirens* (coast redwood)
- *Sequoiadendron giganteum* (sierra redwood)
- *Thuja* spp. (arborvitae)

Tree shapes

When choosing a tree, it is vital to consider what shape it will be – not only when it is young, but when it is fully grown. There are several recognized shapes, but remember that trees are living things, and distinctions between the types are often blurred – some trees might be described as either vase-shaped or globular, for example.

Function of the tree

The first consideration when selecting a tree is to decide what you want to achieve. For example, if you wanted to hide a telephone or utility pole, you could choose from among the numerous columnar, conical, pyramidal or narrow-growing deciduous and coniferous trees as well as some tropical palms.

Once established, the tree would occupy less space than a spreading species, but its habit of growth would provide interest while not having a huge impact on the surrounding planting, apart from competing for light and water. However, if you wanted to block out a house or other large view, a broadly spreading tree would be a more appropriate choice.

Columnar trees

As the name suggests, these trees have a tall, cylindrical, narrow habit with upswept and slightly twisted branches. This growth trait gives them strength as the branches are tightly packed to the trunk.

Columnar trees (also called fastigiate trees) have a clear, dominant central leader and narrow, acutely positioned branches. They are often distinguished by being the same width all the way up, almost to the top, which sometimes spreads slightly or ends in a narrow point.

Plant columnar trees where little canopy spread is required and where a variation in tree line is required to contrast with broadly spreading trees and shrubs. Columnar conifers are often grown to create focal points in Mediterranean-style garden landscapes because they are similar in outline to *Cupressus sempervirens* (Italian cypress).

They can be planted in groups to great effect, and they form unusual-looking avenues where space is limited. They can also be used to frame views and when used as lawn specimens they add formality.

A broadly spreading tree, such as these horse chestnuts, would be ideal for blocking out an unsightly view or for creating a sense of privacy.

This *Acer rubrum* 'Columnare' is a good example of a columnar tree.

Trees with a columnar habit

Acer campestre 'Elsrijk' (field maple)
A. davidii 'Serpentine' (David's maple)
A. platanoides 'Erectum' (Norway maple)
A. rubrum 'Columnare' (red maple)
A. saccharum subsp. *nigrum* 'Monumental' (sugar maple)
A. saccharum subsp. *nigrum* 'Newton Sentry' (sugar maple)
Betula pendula 'Obelisk' (silver birch)
Calocedrus decurrens (incense cedar)
Carpinus betulus 'Frans Fontäne' (hornbeam)
Chamaecyparis lawsoniana cvs. (Lawson's cypress)
Corylus colurna (Turkish hazel)
Crataegus monogyna 'Stricta' (hawthorn)
x *Cupressocyparis leylandii* cvs. (Leyland cypress)
Cupressus sempervirens (Italian cypress)
Eucryphia spp.
Fagus sylvatica 'Dawyck' (Dawyck beech)
Ginkgo biloba 'Fastigiata' (maidenhair tree)
Juniperus chinensis (Chinese juniper)
Koelreuteria paniculata 'Fastigiata' (golden rain tree)
Liquidambar styraciflua 'Slender Silhouette' (sweet gum)
Liriodendron tulipifera 'Fastigiata' (tulip tree)
Pinus sylvestris Fastigiata Group (Scots pine)
Populus nigra 'Italica' (Lombardy poplar)
Pyrus calleryiana (Callery pear)
Robinia pseudoacacia 'Pyramidalis' (false acacia)
Taxodium distichum var. *imbricaria* 'Nutans' (pond cypress)
Taxus baccata 'Fastigiata' (Irish yew)
Tilia platyphyllos 'Fastigiata' (lime)

Cedrus dedora 'Golden Horizon' is a good example of a naturally conical tree.

Thuja plicata (arborvitae) has a typical conical habit, and can also be used for hedging.

Conical and pyramidal trees

These trees look rather like upside down ice-cream cones. They have a less tight habit of growth than columnar or fastigiate trees. Many conifers are naturally conical in shape, as are several broadleaf trees.

The main difference between a conical and a columnar tree is that the spread of the lower branches of a conical tree is wider than that of a columnar tree – 2m (6ft) or more across – and can be as much as one-quarter of the tree's height.

Conical trees can be extremely useful for framing views. They are often used to great effect in avenues and can also provide an attractive contrast when they are planted in combination with a group of broad spreading deciduous species.

Many trees that appear columnar or conical when young can widen in spread as they age as the lower branches increase in length and begin to sag under their own weight.

A pyramidal tree will have a wider spread than both columnar and conical trees – it can be as much as half its height. These trees have a strong central leader. The lower branches are sometimes raised so that other plants can grow underneath, although this can sometimes make the overall shape look somewhat stunted.

Pyramidal trees can be used effectively as specimen trees in lawns and included in mixed plantings to diversify the planting and produce a range of canopy shapes. They also make interesting avenues and can be grown in groups to create a more formal design.

Vase-shaped trees

Small, vase-shaped trees are preferred in some locations and are especially useful in smaller gardens where a spreading tree is required but where lower-canopy space is limited.

Because of their shape, these trees cast greater shade than columnar, conical or pyramidal trees. On the

Tilia platyphyllos (broad-leaved lime) is typical of a broad-spreading pyramidal tree.

This *Taxodium distichum* (bald cypress) is a good example of a narrow, pyramidal tree.

Trees with a conical or pyramidal habit

Abies spp. (fir)
Acer campestre 'Queen Elizabeth' (field maple)
A. x *freemanii* cvs. (Freeman's maple)
A. saccharum cvs. (red maple)
Agathis spp. (kauri pine)
Araucaria spp. (monkey puzzle)
Cedrus atlantica (Atlantic cedar)
C. deodara (deodar cedar)
Chamaecyparis spp. (false cypress)
Cornus nuttallii (Pacific dogwood)
x *Cupressocyparis leylandii* cvs. (Leyland cypress)
Cupressus spp. (cypress)
Ilex x *altaclarensis* cvs. (Highclere holly)
I. aquifolium cvs. (English holly)
I. latifolia
Larix spp. (larch)
Laurus nobilis (bay)
Magnolia grandiflora cvs. (bull bay magnolia)
Oxydendron arboreum (sorrel tree)
Picea spp. (spruce)
Pinus spp. (pine)
Pseudolarix amabilis (golden larch)
Quercus acutissima (sawtooth oak)
Sequoia sempervirens (coast redwood)
Sequoiadendron giganteum (sierra redwood)
Taxodium distichum (swamp cypress)
Thuja spp. (arborvitae)
Thujopsis dolabrata (hiba)
Tilia cordata 'Corinthian' (small-leaved lime)
T. platyphyllos (broad-leaved lime)
T. platyphyllos 'Princess Street' (broad-leaved lime)
T. tomentosa (European white lime)

The multiple branches of *Zelkovia carpinfolia* sweep upwards in a classic vase shape.

Acer 'White Tigress' has a defined vase shape.

plus side, however, they have an attractive, interesting shape, even when small, and cast less shade than a round-headed or weeping tree.

Vase-shaped trees differ from columnar, conical and pyramidal trees in that they lack a central leader. Their multiple branches originate from the trunk and point upwards. The numerous upswept branches are tightly placed and form a canopy with a flat top.

Because of the distinctive branch structure of vase-shaped trees, many of the internal branches can be safely removed to allow views through the tree. They can also be successfully and attractively pruned to allow for electricity or overhead services wires.

Small lower understorey, medium-sized upper understorey and upper-canopy vase-shaped trees are available and can be used in mixed canopy plantings. They are also invaluable as understorey trees in woodland gardens. When they are used in avenues they produce effective 'cathedral' avenues that are clear near the base and arched together higher up, resembling a cathedral arch.

Vase-shaped trees are useful for blocking out unattractive views but they are often less impressive when used as specimens in lawns. This is because their twisted branches can look rather unsightly in winter. However, careful pruning when they are young can help to alleviate this and improve their overall appearance.

Trees with a vase-shaped habit

Acer davidii (David's maple)
A. palmatum (Japanese maple)
A. rubrum (red maple)
A. saccharum (sugar maple)
Cercis siliquastrum (Judas tree)
Cladrastis lutea (yellow wood)
Koelreuteria paniculata (golden rain tree)
Lagerstroemia fauriei
Magnolia x soulangeana (Chinese magnolia)
Malus spp. and cvs. (crab apple)
Parrotia persica (Persian ironwood)
Prunus 'Kanzan' (ornamental cherry)
P. sargentii (Sargent cherry)
Pterocarya stenoptera (wing nut)
Quercus frainetto (Hungarian oak)
Sassafras albidum
Ulmus parvifolia (Chinese elm)
Zelkova serrata 'Green Vase'

Round-headed trees

Of the tree shapes available, this is probably the type most often seen. Round-headed trees are as wide as they are tall and have a symmetrical crown that looks round in silhouette.

These trees cast considerable shade, and can occupy the space that would be taken by several columnar, conical, pyramidal or vase-shaped trees of similar height, though their water and nutrient requirements will be less than those of a group of narrower trees.

Round-headed trees are best used as upper-canopy trees when maximum spread and shade are required. They make good lawn specimens if there is sufficient space for their canopy to develop and enough space surrounding them so that they do not dominate the landscape. Ideally, the nearest tree to them should not be closer than half the height of the larger tree when it is mature.

Round-headed trees can also be used where just a single tree is needed, especially where maximum shade is essential. They are used in avenues or allées only where there is room for their spread, otherwise the avenue may feel very narrow and claustrophobic.

This *Crataegus coccinea* (scarlet haw) is a good example of a typical round-headed tree, and can be used to block out an unsightly view.

Trees with a round-headed habit

Acacia spp. (mimosa/wattle)
Acer campestre (field maple)
A. davidii (David's maple)
A. griseum (paperbark maple)
A. japonica (full-moon maple)
A. platanoides (Norway maple)
A. rufinerve (red-vein maple)
Aesculus spp. (horse chestnut)
Ailanthus altissima (tree of heaven)
Albizia julibrissin (silk tree)
Arbutus unedo (strawberry tree)
Artocarpus altilis (breadfruit)
Betula ermanii (Erman's birch)
Brownea macrophylla (Panama flame tree)
Calophyllum inophyllum (Alexandrian laurel)
Carpinus spp. (hornbeam)
Castanea spp. (sweet chestnut)
Catalpa spp. (bean tree)
Citrus aurantium (Seville orange)
C. x *paradisi* (grapefruit)
Cornus florida cvs. (flowering dogwood)
C. kousa cvs. (kousa dogwood)
Crataegus spp. and cvs. (hawthorn/may)
Davidia involucrata (handkerchief tree)
Dillenia indica (chulta)
Diospyrus spp. (persimmon)
Fagus spp. (beech)
Fraxinus spp. (ash)
Gleditsia spp. (locust)
Grevillea robusta (silky oak)
Juglans spp. (walnut)
Koelreuteria paniculata (golden rain tree)
Laburnum spp. (golden rain)
Liquidambar styraciflua (sweet gum)
Liriodendron tulipifera (tulip tree)
Lithocarpus spp. (tan oak)
Magnolia stellata (star magnolia)
Malus spp. and cvs. (crab apple)
Morus spp. (mulberry)
Nyssa spp. (tupelo)
Platanus spp. (plane)
Plumeria spp. (frangipani)
Prunus spp. and cvs. (cherry)
Psidium spp. (guava)
Quercus spp. (oak)
Robinia spp. (locust/false acacia)
Sophora japonica (Japanese pagoda tree)
Tilia spp. (lime)

Globular trees

Trees with a globular habit are similar to round-headed trees but they are slightly wider than they are tall. Unlike round-headed trees, the overall shape, not just the canopy, is round. Globular trees are broadly spreading and cast more shade than round-headed trees. They are widely used as upper-storey and upper understorey trees where wide shapes are desired. Their spreading canopy makes them unsuitable for use as lawn specimens or in avenues and allées, but they can be used in groups as landscape trees in parkland.

Liquidambar styraciflua 'Variegata' is a widely grown globular tree.

Sorbus aria 'Lutescens' is a deciduous globular tree from Europe.

Trees with a globular habit

Acer macrophyllum (Oregon maple)
A. platanoides (Norway maple)
A. pseudoplatanus (sycamore)
A. sterculiaceum (Himalayan maple)
Aesculus x *carnea* (red horse chestnut)
A. indica (Indian horse chestnut)
A. turbinata (Japanese horse chestnut)
Amelanchier spp. (Juneberry)
Brachychiton acerifolius (flame tree)
Carpinus betulus (hornbeam)
Cercidiphyllum spp. (katsura)
Cercis spp. (Judas tree/redbud)
Cornus mas (Cornelian cherry)
C. officinalis (dogwood)
Cotinus spp. (smoke tree)
Eriobotrya japonica (loquat)
Ficus spp. (fig)
Liquidambar styraciflua (sweet gum)
Ligustrum lucidum (Japanese privet)
Magnolia x *soulangeana*
Myrtus communis (myrtle)
Parrotia persica (Persian ironwood)
Quercus cerris (Turkey oak)
Q. ilex (holm oak)
Q. robur (common oak)
Q. suber (cork oak)
Sorbus aria (whitebeam)
S. megalocarpa
S. thibetica
Taxus baccata (yew)

Ficus benghalensis (banyan) is a fast-growing, globular tree that is widely used in the tropics for avenues or for street planting.

Weeping trees

Often giving a rather shaggy appearance, weeping trees have long branches that hang downwards. Most weeping trees are cultivars – the form is less common among wild species.

Because the stems and foliage often touch the ground, it is difficult to grow other plants below weeping trees. For this reason, they are best used as focal points in the garden or as lawn specimens, where their beautiful habit and foliage can be fully appreciated. They also provide a wonderful opportunity for children to enjoy having a secret hiding place under the branches.

Trees with a weeping habit

Ailanthus altissima 'Pendula' (tree of heaven)
Alnus incana 'Pendula' (weeping grey alder)
Betula nigra 'Cascade Falls' (weeping river birch)
B. pendula 'Youngii' (Young's weeping birch)
Cassia fistulosa (golden shower tree)
Cedrus deodara (deodar cedar)
Cercidiphyllum japonicum f. *pendulum* (weeping katsura)
Cercis canadensis var. *texensis* 'Traveller' (weeping eastern redbud)
Chamaecyparis lawsoniana 'Intertexta' (Lawson's cypress)
Cupressus cashmeriana (Kashmir cypress)
Eucalyptus coccifera (Tasmanian snow gum)
Fagus sylvatica 'Pendula' (weeping common beech)
Ficus benjamina (weeping fig)
Fraxinus excelsior 'Pendula' (weeping ash)
Juniperus recurva (Himalayan weeping juniper)
Larix decidua 'Pendula' (weeping larch)
Malus 'Royal Beauty' (weeping crab apple)
Morus alba 'Pendula' (weeping mulberry)
Nyssa sylvatica 'Autumn Cascade' (weeping tupelo)
Pinus strobus 'Pendula' (weeping white pine)
Robinia x *margaretta* 'Pink Cascade'
Salix babylonica (weeping willow)
Tilia tomentosa 'Petiolaris' (weeping silver lime)

Although many conifers are grown for their conical habit, a number, such as this *Chamaecyparis nootkansensis* 'Pendula', have beautiful weeping branches.

The foliage of *Picea breweriana* (Brewer's spruce) hangs like curtains from its weeping branches.

Prostrate trees

Trees that do not grow upright are known as prostrate trees. They lie along the ground and can be used to create focal points in the garden. They are useful for planting over banks where their strange shapes provide ground cover. Prostrate trees can also be trained up a framework, rather like a wall-shrub.

Horizontally branched trees

The branches on horizontally branched trees grow at an angle of 90 degrees to the trunk and give a layered appearance. *Cedrus libani* (cedar of Lebanon) and *Cornus controversa* (table dogwood) are good examples. Their winter silhouette is distinctive and can be dramatically enhanced by pruning to encourage the layered effect. Horizontally branched trees are best used as focal points or specimen trees in lawns, but they can be included in mixed planting if there is space for them to grow unimpeded by other trees.

Low-branched and feathered trees

Many shade-tolerant trees do not shed their lower branches with age, often retaining them down to the ground. Although many nurseries prune the lower branches off to create a clear trunk (standard trees), some will not, and these are sold as feathered trees.

Feathered trees usually have a less contrived shape than standard trees and are best used as lawn specimens and in avenues and allées where, in order to create a tunnelled effect, trees reaching down or close to the ground are required. Many coniferous trees look more natural when they are grown this way, although the denseness of the lower branches means that nothing can be grown beneath them.

Cornus controversa 'Variegata' (pagoda dogwood) has horizontal branches, shown here in full bloom.

This *Araucaria araucana* has been feathered at the nursery so that it retains its lower branches. Here it is used to good effect as a focal point specimen in a lawn.

Choosing trees

Trees are among the longest-living organisms on our planet – which can make it a bit daunting when choosing one for your garden. Deciding what you need in terms of size, shape, colour and seasonal interest, as well as taking into account soil and climate conditions, only adds to the difficulties.

The answer is to do your homework, which is not as arduous as it sounds. Visiting a nearby arboretum or park is usually helpful, as you will see full-grown trees that are suited to the local conditions, and they should be labelled with their names. Looking at your neighbours' gardens will also give you an idea of what is likely to do well in your own. To further ensure the trees you choose are suitable, check out their requirements and potential size in a reference book, or on the internet.

Once armed with this information, you can go to your local garden centre or nursery to further whittle down your selection, based on availability and price.

With so many different types of tree to choose from, you may well find that you are spoilt for choice when you visit a nursery. It is important that you take the shape, colour and ultimate size of the tree into account to ensure you buy the right one for your garden.

Researching trees

Buying a tree for your garden requires careful planning. Most of us have space for only a limited number, and many of the trees we might like to grow will simply be too large for the average garden. However, there will still be an enormous range of possibilities. When making your choice, remember that, all being well, any tree you plant will be an important feature in your garden for many years to come.

Not only are arboreta invaluable resources for scientists, but they are also popular attractions for those with a more general interest in trees.

Arboreta

The most common form of tree collection where you can start your research is an arboretum, which is a botanical collection of trees grown mainly for their scientific and educational value. Arboreta, like botanical gardens, originally were – and still are to some extent – used to help sort out the problems with tree names and the classification of trees.

Many universities and botanic gardens throughout the world have specialized tree collections within their grounds or even a separate arboretum. These tree collections are invaluable when looking at the growth, habit and form of specific trees, but until relatively recently were not a great deal of help when looking at the aesthetics of trees in the landscape.

However, to increase the interest in rather obscure tree collections there has been considerable new landscaping in order to display trees in numerous innovative ways. These include trees that are grouped by their countries of origin; trees with special adaptations, such as tolerance of heavy or waterlogged soils or urban environments; trees with exceptional autumn colour, flowers and habit; and rare trees.

Any of these themes can be implemented in the garden environment, but most need careful planning as the most attractive trees often do not make the most attractive landscape unless carefully arranged.

An arboretum is, strictly, a collection of trees, although many also include other woody plants, such as shrubs and climbers. A pinetum is an arboretum specializing in coniferous plants. Botanic gardens contain plants other than trees.

Botanic gardens

A botanic garden is a collection of plants amassed by a particular institution for the purposes of research and public education. Each may specialize in a different group of trees, but it will also include a number of commonly grown and some more unusual plants. These can be organized in numerous ways, such as by plant family, geography, type of ornamental features (tree shape, season of interest, flower, fruit or foliage) and so on.

Botanic gardens give an opportunity to compare different trees that may be growing near each other. They also have expert staff who can advise you on your choice.

Sources of information

Nursery and some larger garden centres are good places to start when researching trees, although they may only stock a limited range of small trees. However, they are likely to stock books and pamphlets, and you may be able to speak to an expert with local knowledge of the best trees to grow in your area.

A vast amount of data is available on the internet, including images, comprehensive details about the tree and its ideal growing conditions. Reading through professionally run websites allows you to view the trees that interest you and compare them with others.

Learning about trees

Both botanic gardens and arboreta have the advantage that the plants are labelled with their botanic and common name. Both organizations usually also maintain records, including information on when each tree was planted so that you can tell how tall and wide it has grown in a given period. They also often produce leaflets and handouts, have regular guided walks and may have web-based plant records that you can consult from home.

Parks and other public spaces are good places to begin learning to recognize different trees, although these trees are rarely labelled, so you need to know what you are looking for before you see them.

Tree collections should remain the main goal of those who wish to collect trees simply for their individual beauty – and who have sufficient space to amass a sizeable tree collection. The rest of us have to rely on visits to gardens, parks and woodland to appreciate trees in profusion.

Take a visit to your local park to see what sort of tree you want. If you have trouble identifying an unnamed tree, the park authorities will help you.

Choosing the right tree

Selecting a new tree is not something that should be undertaken lightly. It is not like shopping for a refrigerator or kettle because your new purchase is alive and will require care and attention for many years to come.

Factors to consider

Before you choose a tree, you need to consider many different factors so that you can draw up a shortlist of potential candidates. Whether you are adding a single specimen or turning your entire garden over to trees, the first step is to assess the conditions in your garden. Aim to build up a comprehensive overview of your existing garden before you even think about choosing a tree.

Once you have answered these questions, there are then other, less practical and more aesthetic considerations. Trees have so many qualities – shape and habit of growth, leaf colour and form, flowers, fruit and bark – that it can be difficult to know which attribute is most important.

Before you decide what species of tree you are going to buy, it is a good idea to ask yourself some simple questions, making a note of the answers so that you can easily find the best tree for your garden.

The importance of scale

Before you base your decision about a new tree for your garden on a particular species' aesthetic attributes, consider its ultimate size, which is not just its height but also its spread. Many trees have broadly spreading crowns, which cast dense shade under which little else will grow. In a small garden in particular, height and spread must be your first considerations.

Knowing the height and spread of a tree will help you make the right choice. A tree should blend in to the scale of your existing plants and with the wider garden landscape.

All plants grow more quickly in a climate where their growth is not affected by late spring frosts, where

Robinia pseudoacacia 'Frisia' is a beautiful tree that is suitable for small to medium gardens.

Important questions to ask yourself

What is my soil like? Is it:

- Acidic?
- Alkaline?
- Neutral?
- Free-draining?
- Waterlogged?

Why do I want to plant a tree?

- For shape?
- To screen an object?
- To reduce noise?
- To absorb pollution?
- For a windbreak?
- For decorative effect (fruit, flower, foliage or bark)?
- For protection or privacy?
- As a focal point?
- As a habitat for wildlife?

What shape of tree do I want?

- Broadly spreading?
- Upright?
- Conical?
- One for producing a special effect by pruning (coppicing, pollarding)?
- Deciduous or evergreen or with exotic foliage, like a palm?

What size of tree do I want?

- How much space do I have?
- How big are my existing plants and trees?

What are my location and site like?

- What type of climate do I have?
- Is the site protected or in a frost pocket?
- Is the garden exposed to wind?
- What is the surrounding tree cover like and do I want to blend a new tree in with existing trees?
- How do we use the garden and how will we use it in the future?
- How far will it be from the house and other buildings?
- How far will it be from services (electricity and utility cables, drains and paths)

How much money am I prepared to spend, both buying and caring for the tree?

How much time do I want to spend caring for the tree?

there is adequate rainfall throughout the growing season and where they are growing in fertile, moisture-retentive soil. In such conditions a tree could be expected to attain its maximum height and spread when its reaches maturity.

In contrast, the same tree might grow only half as tall if it was grown in a nutrient-poor, free-draining soil, with below average rainfall in a location where it was not fully hardy and the new growth was killed by frost in spring.

The heights and spreads given for different species featured in the Directory section are only a guide and are given on the assumption that the tree is growing in the optimum conditions. If possible, visit a park or arboretum to view examples of the trees that interest you before you buy.

Another factor to consider is the space available. If a tree is grown as a lawn specimen it does not have to compete with nearby trees for light and nutrients, and it would be more likely to develop a balanced crown. However, when the same species is grown in a group, it will have to compete with its neighbours so may not grow as wide.

Morus alba 'Pendula' (weeping mulberry) is a popular ornamental tree with a low-growing, weeping habit that is ideal for a small space.

Small garden trees

If the space in your garden is limited, you may find that only a small, slow-growing species can be comfortably accommodated. Most trees look best when allowed to grow freely and retain their natural shape, but you might choose a species that will respond well to annual pruning or pollarding to restrict its size. In very small gardens, it might be best to consider a large shrub instead of a tree.

Small garden trees can also be used as understorey trees, where there are already larger trees forming an upper canopy. You might have a tall top canopy from a number of established trees and existing shrub cover at a lower level. An intermediate tree canopy will introduce a more diverse range of plants, providing an additional flowering layer or autumn colour theme. It will also provide shade and a more balanced planting scheme.

Trees for small gardens

Abies koreana (Korean fir)
Acacia dealbata (mimosa)
Acer japonicum (full-moon maple)
A. palmatum (Japanese maple)
Arbutus unedo (strawberry tree)
Banksia spp.
Bauhinia spp. (mountain ebony)
Betula pendula 'Youngii' (Young's weeping birch)
Bismarckia nobilis (noble palm)
Calliandra spp. (powder puff tree)
Callistemon spp. (bottlebrush)
Calophyllum inophyllum (Alexandrian laurel)
Caryota spp. (fishtail palm)
Cercis canadensis (eastern redbud)
C. siliquastrum (Judas tree)
Citrus spp.
Cladrastis spp.
Cornus florida (flowering dogwood)
Crataegus spp. (hawthorn, most)
Erythrina spp. (coral tree)
Grevillea spp. (spider flower)
Ilex spp. (holly, most)
Koelreuteria paniculata (golden rain tree)
Lagerstroemia spp.
Livistona chinensis (Chinese fan palm)
Magnolia spp.
Malus spp. and cvs. (crab apple, most)
Oxydendrum arboreum (sorrel tree)
Plumeria spp. (frangipani)
Prunus spp. (ornamental cherry, most)
Psidium spp. (guava)
Sabal palmetto (cabbage palmetto)
Schefflera elegantissima (false aralia)
Sorbus spp. (mountain ash, most)
Stewartia spp. (most)
Tecoma stans (yellow elder)
Trachycarpus fortunei (Chusan palm)

Medium-sized garden trees

This group includes species of garden trees that grow between 15 and 30m (50–100ft) tall. Trees that are at the upper end of the medium-size height range can be included to provide the top canopy, whereas the lower growing species can be used as intermediate or lower-canopy trees to create a succession of height, interest and habitat.

Trees for medium-sized gardens

Acacia spp. (mimosa/wattle)
Acer platanoides (Norway maple)
Aesculus flava (yellow buckeye)
Albizia spp. (silk tree)
Betula ermanii (Erman's birch)
Carpinus betulus (common hornbeam)
Catalpa bignonioides (Indian bean tree)
Cercidiphyllum japonicum (katsura tree)
Clusia major (autograph tree)
Corylus colurna (Turkish hazel)
Davidia involucrata (handkerchief tree)
Fraxinus spp. (ash, many)
Ginkgo biloba (maidenhair tree)
Gleditsia spp. (many)
Liquidambar styraciflua (sweet gum)
Magnolia oborata (Japanese big-leaf magnolia)
Metrosideros spp. (rata)
Phoenix spp. (date palm)
Tabebuia spp.

Beware the tree you choose. This *Pinus sylvestris* (Scots pine) is extremely tall when fully grown.

Large and parkland trees

Trees that grow to 30m (100ft) or more are suitable only for the largest of gardens. They often form the backbone of parkland planting and can be used individually or in small groups in extensive landscapes. Sometimes a group of three or five will be used to create the impression of a single specimen when viewed from a distance.

Many of these trees are extremely long-lived, exceeding 150 years of age, so their positioning requires the utmost care. In large urban gardens, such trees would form the upper canopy, with medium-sized trees forming the intermediate canopy and small trees the lower canopy.

While few gardeners have the space for full-grown specimens, some choose to plant them anyway, to enjoy them while they are small and then transplant them to a more suitable location.

Trees that grow quickly

When they are grown in ideal conditions some trees can, in just a few years, reach a significant height, bringing a degree of maturity to even a young garden. This ability to establish and grow quickly also makes this group of trees valuable as nurse trees, which are grown to protect and provide shelter for the 'real' garden trees while they establish. Nurse trees are generally removed once they have completed their work as they will quickly compete for light, water and nutrients with the trees that they are protecting.

Fast-growing trees can also be used to provide windbreaks and shelter-belts. They are also effective at creating quick shade and can, therefore, be used as upper-storey, shade trees.

Trees for large gardens

Abies grandis (giant fir)
Aesculus hippocastanum (horse chestnut)
Agathis australis (kauri pine)
Araucaria araucana (monkey puzzle)
Carya spp. (hickory, most)
Cedrus libani (cedar of Lebanon)
Cinnamomum spp. (camphor tree)
Eucalyptus spp. (gum tree, many)
Ficus benghalensis (banyan)
F. elastica (India rubber tree)
Jacaranda mimosifolia
Liriodendron tulipifera (tulip tree)
Pinus sylvestris (Scots pine)
Platanus x *hispanica* (London plane)
Quercus spp. (oak)
Roystonea regia (Cuban royal palm)
Sequoia sempervirens (coast redwood)
Sequoiadendron giganteum (sierra redwood)
Tilia x *europaea* (common lime)

Fast-growing trees

Abies spp. (silver fir)
Aesculus spp. (horse chestnut)
Aleurites moluccana (candlenut)
Alnus spp. (alder)
Betula spp. (birch)
Calocedrus decurrens (incense cedar)
Calodendron capense (Cape chestnut)
Calophyllum inophyllum (Alexandrian laurel)
Catalpa bignonioides (Indian bean tree)
Cedrus atlantica Glauca Group
Chamaecyparis lawsoniana (Lawson's cypress)
x *Cupressocyparis leylandii* (Leyland cypress)
Eucalyptus spp. (gum tree)
Fagus spp. (beech)
Jacaranda mimosifolia
Liquidambar styraciflua (sweet gum)
Metasequoia glyptostroboides (dawn redwood)
Olea europaea (European olive)
Paulownia tomentosa (empress tree)
Pinus palustris (pitch pine)
Platanus spp. (plane)
Populus spp. (poplar)
Pterocarya stenoptera (wing nut)
Quercus spp. (oak)
Robinia pseudoacacia 'Frisia'
Salix spp. (willow)
Sassafras albidum
Sequoiadendron giganteum (sierra redwood)
Thuja plicata (western red cedar)
Tilia spp. (lime)

Nurse trees

Nurse species provide shade and protection so choicer trees can develop below their rapidly growing crowns. It is their speed of growth rather than their ultimate height that is the important factor. They often do well in less than favourable conditions. Nurse species should be removed once the main trees have developed and no longer require protection.

Acer platanoides is a fast-growing tree that will thrive in nutrient-poor soil. It provides quick shade and is a good nurse tree.

Shape and habit

One of the first considerations is the shape of a tree, which must fit into the overall garden landscape (see Tree shapes, pages 34–41). Fastigiate, columnar and upright-growing trees, such as *Taxus baccata* 'Fastigiata', are excellent for hiding narrow objects, such as telephone or utility poles. Trees like *Quercus robur* f. *fastigiata* or *Cupressus sempervirens* Stricta Group can produce a tropical feel if they are planted with yuccas and palms.

Pendulous or weeping trees bring a graceful silhouette to a landscape. Round-headed trees bring massive green outlines and their trunks create interesting architectural patterns that change during the day as the sun gives way to shade.

Evergreen conifers with a conical shape conjure images of snow-covered mountains. Such trees require a fairly large garden so they do not quickly grow out of scale and become too dominant.

Palms can often be difficult to accommodate in traditional temperate landscapes, as their bold foliage and distinctive outlines have a tropical feel, reminiscent of sunny, sandy beaches on deserted tropical islands; a tropicana landscape that would not suit every garden.

Aesthetic considerations

Wherever possible, especially in a small garden, the aim should be to choose a tree that offers as much year-round interest as possible.

For example, *Trachycarpus fortunei* (Chusan palm) has amazing architectural foliage compared to many evergreens. In spring the palm produces large panicles of bright yellow flowers, followed by clusters of blue-black fruits. As the main stem matures it becomes covered with a matted, fibrous material. In a mild climate this would be an ideal candidate if you are looking for a small, ornamental tree for year-round interest.

Eriobotrya japonica (loquat) will grow massive ovate leaves if it is coppiced.

Trees with architectural foliage

- *Acer* x *conspicuum* 'Elephant's Ear'
- *A. macrophyllum* (Oregon maple)
- *A. pensylvanicum* (striped maple)
- *A. sterculiaceum* (Himalayan maple)
- *Aesculus hippocastanum* (horse chestnut)
- *Artocarpus altilis* (breadfruit)
- *Bismarckia nobilis* (noble palm)
- *Butia capitata* (pindo palm)
- *Caryota* spp. (fishtail palm)
- *Catalpa bignonioides* (Indian bean tree)
- *C. bignonioides* 'Aurea'
- *C. bignonioides* 'Variegata'
- *Chamaerops humilis* (dwarf fan palm)
- *Cryptomeria japonica* 'Lobbii'
- *Dillenia indica* (chulta)
- *Eriobotrya japonica* (loquat)
- *Ficus* spp. (fig)
- *Licuala* spp. (palas)
- *Livistona* spp. (fountain palm)
- *Magnolia delavayi*
- *M. grandiflora* (bull bay magnolia)
- *Paulownia* spp.
- *Phoenix* spp.
- *Pinus coulteri* (big cone pine)
- *P. palustris* (pitch pine)
- *P. patula* (Mexican weeping pine)
- *Pterocarya stenoptera* (wing nut)
- *Roystonea* spp. (royal palm)
- *Sabal* spp. (palmetto)
- *Schefflera* spp.
- *Trachycarpus* spp.

Architectural foliage

As well as beautiful flowers or edible fruits, unusual and architectural foliage should be a consideration when you are selecting a new tree. This type of foliage increases the level of contrast in the garden and, if the tree is carefully positioned, can create a dramatic and breathtaking impression. Architectural foliage is most commonly a characteristic of trees used for lawn specimens or as focal points in the garden.

These trees are distinguished by large leaves, which are attractive in their own right. Most palms fall into this category, and they also associate well with other large-leaved plants to create a lush, exotic effect even in a temperate climate.

Some trees, such as *Paulownia tomentosa* (empress tree) and *Catalpa bignonioides* (Indian bean tree), can be coppiced to a small framework of branches. This hard pruning encourages the growth of large leaves, creating an architectural tree.

No tree is more distinctive in the landscape than the palms, with their large architectural leaves held high above their bare stems. They are widely used as upper-canopy trees in a tropical landscape.

Attracting wildlife

Garden trees and shrubs that provide food and cover are sought out by many birds and mammals, both resident and migratory. A mixture of deciduous and evergreen material provides valuable cover for many animals, especially if dense conifers are incorporated into the planting.

Evergreen species often attract winter songbirds and provide valuable shelter for game birds, and their food can be supplemented by bird feeders placed in or near the trees. Conifers and thorny bushes and trees are used by summer visitors and residents alike as safe nesting and roosting sites.

Trees and shrubs that provide food in the form of seeds, nuts and fruit are highly desirable, and those that last into the winter and possibly into the following spring are preferred. Included in this group are *Malus* species and cultivars (crab apple) and *Sorbus* species (mountain ash).

Trees that fruit in spring, summer and early autumn include *Morus* spp. (mulberry), *Prunus* spp. (cherry) and *Cornus* (dogwood). Conifers that hold their seeds in semi-loose cones will attract seed-eaters and also provide winter nesting sites.

Many trees provide invaluable shelter and food for different species of birds and other wildlife during the cold months of winter.

Trees such as *Quercus* (oak), *Juglans* (walnut), *Carya* (hickory), *Corylus* (hazel) and *Fagus* (beech), which produce hard winter nuts (masts), attract large seed-eating birds and small mammals.

Standing dead wood in trees, including snags and trees with dead tops or limbs, will attract many different species of animal, so don't always be in a hurry to tidy up dead wood. These trees furnish cavity nest sites for many songbirds, squirrels or bats, as well as providing insect larvae for woodpeckers.

Trees to encourage wildlife

Aesculus hippocastanum (horse chestnut)
Betula alleghaniensis (yellow birch)
B. lenta (cherry birch)
B. nigra (black birch)
B. pendula (silver birch)
Bismarckia nobilis (noble palm)
Butia capitata (pindo palm)
Carpinus betulus (common hornbeam)
C. caroliniana (American hornbeam)
Carya illinoinensis (pecan)
Caryota spp. (fishtail palm)
Castanea dentata (American sweet chestnut)
C. sativa (sweet chestnut)
Catalpa bignonioides (Indian bean tree)
Chamaerops humilis (dwarf fan palm)
Corylus colurna (Turkish hazel)
C. jacquemontii
Crataegus spp. (hawthorn)
Dillenia indica (chulta)
Eucalyptus spp. (gum tree)
Fagus (American beech)
F. orientalis (oriental beech)
F. sylvatica (common beech)
Ficus spp. (fig)
Juglans regia (common walnut)
Licuala spp. (palas)
Livistona spp. (fountain palm)
Magnolia spp. and cvs.
Malus spp. and cvs. (crab apple)
Morus spp. (mulberry)
Olea europaea (European olive)
Phoenix spp. (date palm)
Plumeria spp. (frangipani)
Psidium guajava (common guava)
Punica granatum (pomegranate)
Pyrus spp. (pear)
Quercus spp. (oak)
Roystonea spp. (royal palm)
Sabal spp. (palmetto)
Sassafras albidum
Sorbus spp. (mountain ash)
Syzygium spp. (wild rose)
Tilia spp. (lime)
Trachycarpus spp.

Trees for colourful foliage

When you are selecting ornamental trees for your garden, it's important to think about seasonal variation. With a little pruning, it's possible to have colourful-looking trees throughout the year.

The beauty of trees

Trees can provide a breathtaking array of colour in the garden and can dramatically enhance and support the shrub and herbaceous plantings below, acting as protection and a foil for these small plants. Colourful foliage and flowers are important, of course, but trees also bring fruits, shape, texture and bark and stem colour through the gardening year.

Trees with yellow foliage

Abies pinsapo 'Aurea' (Spanish fir)
Acer campestre 'Postelense'
A. cappadocicum 'Aureum'
A. negundo 'Kelly's Gold'
A. palmatum 'Sango Kaku'
A. pseudoplatanus 'Brilliantissimum'
Aesculus hippocastanum 'Hampton Court Gold'
Alnus glutinosa 'Aurea'
Betula pendula 'Golden Cloud'
Catalpa bignonioides 'Aurea'
Cedrus deodara 'Aurea'
C. deodara 'Cream Puff'
Chamaecyparis pisifera 'Filifera Aurea'
x *Cupressocyparis leylandii* 'Castlewellan'
x *C. leylandii* 'Gold Rider'
Fagus sylvatica 'Dawyck Gold'
Gleditsia triacanthos 'Sunburst'
Juniperus chinensis 'Aurea'
Metasequoia glyptostroboides 'Gold Rush'
Picea orientalis 'Aurea'
Pinus sylvestris Aurea Group
Populus x *jackii* 'Aurora'
Robinia pseudoacacia 'Frisia'
Thuja plicata 'Atrovirens'
T. plicata 'Irish Gold'
Thujopsis dolobrata 'Aurea'
Tilia platyphyllos 'Aurea'
Tsuga canadensis 'Golden Splendor'
Ulmus x *hollandica* 'Dampieri Aurea'

Foliage factors

The leaves of a tree are as distinctive as the trees themselves. They can vary from the glossy, deep green, long-tipped leaves of *Ficus benjamina* (weeping fig), to the massive deciduous leaves of *Magnolia macrophylla* (great-leaved magnolia, umbrella tree), which can grow to 1m (3ft) long and which is easily damaged by strong winds.

When you are choosing a tree for its foliage, you need to consider what the leaves' shape, size, texture and colour will be in spring, summer, autumn and winter. You also need to decide whether you want an evergreen or a deciduous species. These factors should be assessed in conjunction with the position the tree will occupy in the garden and the plants that will be near it.

Leaf shape can vary from entire (undivided and without teeth) and palmate (palm-like), to pinnate (feather-like). With such a range

Metasequoia glyptostroboides 'Gold Rush' has lovely yellow foliage in spring, which fades to yellow-green during the summer.

Lithocarpus edulis (tan oak) has lovely dark green, glossy foliage and edible acorns.

on offer, it is easy to achieve interest by simply combining several different foliage shapes.

Foliage colour is also highly diverse. Some trees produce spectacular spring foliage, such as the salmon pink foliage of *Acer pseudoplatanus* 'Brilliantissimum', the bright yellow of *Robinia pseudoacacia* 'Frisia' or the purple of *Prunus cerasifera* 'Pissardii' (purple-leaved plum).

Brightly coloured or glossy foliage can be used to highlight a dark part of the garden with a refreshing splash of colour, while dark foliage, such as the purple hues, can be used as a foil for other trees or as a statement of an individual specimen.

Acer palmatum var. *dissectum* in its various forms is grown for the rich colour of its leaves.

Colourful foliage

Trees with unusually coloured foliage bring a welcome variation into the garden, but some restraint may be required as too much colour can look unnatural and be overpowering. However, combinations of trees with purple and yellow or silver and blue foliage can make a stunning display when there is sufficient greenery around them to provide a calming foil.

The lime green foliage of *Pseudolarix amabilis* turns intense yellow in autumn.

Yellow foliage

Trees with yellow foliage bring vibrancy to a mixed garden or border planting. A tree with yellow foliage can be a beautiful focal point when surrounded by green-leaved trees.

The lack of green pigment in the leaf means that some yellow-leaved trees are susceptible to sun scorch and should be planted in light dappled shade to protect the delicate leaves. Some yellow leaves turn lime green in deep shade. However, not all yellow-leaved trees are light-shy, and many will grow well in full sun.

As with variegated leaves, those with yellow foliage are slower growing than the green-leaved forms of the same species and may require more care after planting.

Purple foliage

Nearly all trees with purple foliage are deciduous; there are just a few evergreen species. In some forms the purple can change to green-purple during the summer. Use purple-leaved trees carefully. If they are overplanted they can look like voids in the landscape and give the impression of a 'purple space'. To avoid this, position them near plants with yellow or variegated foliage or use as lawn specimens.

Trees with purple foliage

Acacia baileyana 'Purpurea'
Acer cappadocicum 'Rubrum'
A. palmatum 'Bloodgood'
A. palmatum var. *dissectum* 'Garnet'
A. palmatum var. *dissectum* 'Inaba-shidare'
A. platanoides 'Emerald Lustre'
A. platanoides 'Schwedleri'
A. pseudoplatanus Purpureum Group
Betula pendula 'Purpurea'
Catalpa x *erubescens* 'Purpurea'
Cercis canadensis 'Forest Pansy'
Fagus sylvatica 'Dawyck Purple'
Gleditsia triacanthos 'Rubylace'
Juglans regia 'Purpurea'
Prunus cerasifera 'Pissardii' (purple-leaved plum)
Robinia x *slavinii* 'Purple Robe'

Eucalyptus dalrympleana (mountain gum) is grown for its attractive silver-blue leaves, clusters of flowers and mottled bark.

The leaves of *Eucalyptus cordata* (silver gum) are leathery and silver-blue so they reflect the sunlight.

Silver and blue foliage

The highest proportion of trees with silver and blue foliage is conifers. The brightness of the blue or silvery shoots is often more noticeable on new growth in spring and early summer. The colour is also enhanced in full sunlight, so these trees are best planted in open positions where they will receive as much direct sun as possible. They are often grown as lawn specimens.

Trees with silver and blue foliage

Abies concolor 'Candicans'
Acacia dealbata (silver wattle)
Aleurites moluccana (candlenut)
Bismarckia nobilis (noble palm)
Butia capitata (pindo palm)
Cedrus atlantica Glauca Group
C. deodara (deodar)
C. deodara 'Shalimar'
C. libani (cedar of Lebanon)
Chamaecyparis lawsoniana spp.
Chamaerops humilis var. *argentea* (dwarf fan palm)
x *Cupressocyparis leylandii* 'Naylor's Blue'
x *C. leylandii* 'Silver Dust'
Cupressus sempervirens Stricta Group
Eucalyptus spp. (gum tree)
Fitzroya cupressoides (Patagonian cypress)
Livistona spp. (fountain palm)
Phoenix spp.
Picea pungens (Colorado spruce)
P. pungens 'Hoopsii'
P. pungens 'Koster'
Pinus sylvestris (Scots pine)
P. densiflora (Japanese red pine)
P. strobus (Eastern white pine)
Pyrus salicifolia 'Pendula' (willow-leaved pear)
Roystonea spp. (royal palm)
Sabal spp. (palmetto)
Sequoiadendron giganteum 'Glaucum'
Trachycarpus spp.
Tsuga mertensiana (mountain hemlock)
Washingtonia spp.

Variegated foliage

Tree flowers tend to last only a couple of weeks, but variegated foliage lasts much longer and can provide year-round interest. The leaves of this type of tree can be green, edged with white or yellow; mottled green with white or green; or white and yellow. They tend to be slower growing than trees with all-green foliage, which makes them suitable for small gardens.

You should use trees with variegated foliage in moderation to avoid a messy, confused appearance. They are best positioned where they offer a dramatic contrast against a background of plain green or purple-leaved trees. Some variegated foliage can be susceptible to sun scorch and requires light, dappled shade for best results.

One of the main drawbacks of trees with variegated foliage is that they are susceptible to reversion, which happens when a stem grows

The leaves of *Ilex* x *altaclerensis* 'Golden King' have green centres and bright gold margins.

The variegated leaves of *Ilex aquifolium* 'Golden Queen' have strong golden-yellow edges, making it a desirable small garden tree.

with plain green leaves that contain more chlorophyll than the variegated leaves. Because chlorophyll controls the food-making activity in plants, all-green leaves are stronger and grow more quickly than the stems with variegated leaves, and they soon outgrow the variegated portion of the tree.

Any all-green shoots on a variegated plant should be pruned out. As a rule, evergreen trees with variegated foliage are more tolerant of sunlight than deciduous trees with variegated foliage, which may be more prone to scorch in spring when the new leaves appear. Once fully formed, the risk is reduced.

The new leaves of *Liquidambar styraciflua* 'Variegata' are edged with cream in spring, before becoming flushed with pink in the summer.

Trees with variegated foliage

- *Acer campestre* 'Carnival'
- *A. negundo* 'Flamingo'
- *A. negundo* 'Variegata'
- *A. platanoides* 'Drummondii'
- *A. pseudoplatanus* 'Simon-Louis-Frères'
- *A. rufinerve* 'Hatsuyuki'
- *A.* 'Silver Cardinal'
- *Bauhinia* spp. (mountain ebony)
- *Castanea sativa* 'Albomarginata'
- *Catalpa bignonioides* 'Variegata'
- *Citrus limon* 'Variegata'
- *Cornus controversa* 'Variegata'
- *C. florida* 'Rainbow'
- *Erythrina* spp. (coral tree)
- *Ficus benjamina* 'Variegata'
- *Ficus elastica* cvs.
- *Ginkgo biloba* Variegata Group
- *Ilex aquifolium* cvs.
- *I.* x *altaclerensis* cvs.
- *Liquidambar styraciflua* 'Variegata'
- *Liriodendron tulipifera* 'Aureomarginatum'
- *L. tulipifera* 'Mediopictum'
- *Melia azedarach* 'Jade Snowflake'

Trees for seasonal interest

All trees produce flowers, but we tend to value most those that provide colourful, spectacular or unusual blossom or fruits that last for a long time.

Spring and summer flowers

Most deciduous garden trees flower in spring and summer in response to increasing temperatures and light levels. The variety in size, shape, colour and scent of the flowers of garden trees is quite remarkable, and with careful planning it is possible to have a succession of blooms from early spring to late summer.

In temperate areas, late spring frosts sometimes damage flower buds or the flowers themselves, so take care when siting early-flowering trees – early morning sun will increase any frost damage.

Trees for spring flowers

Acacia dealbata (mimosa)
A. baileyana
Acer pycnanthum (Japanese red maple)
Aesculus 'Dallimorei'
A. hippocastanum (horse chestnut)
A. turbinata (Japanese horse chestnut)
Aesculus x *carnea* (red horse chestnut)
Bauhinia spp. (mountain ebony)
Calliandra spp. (powder puff tree)
Callistemon spp. (bottlebrush)
Calophyllum inophyllum (Alexandrian laurel)
Cassia spp. (shower tree)
Cercis canadensis (eastern redbud)
C. canadensis var. *texensis*
C. siliquastrum (Judas tree)
Clusia major (autograph tree)
Cornus florida (flowering dogwood)
C. nuttallii (Pacific dogwood)
Davidia involucrata (handkerchief tree)
Dillenia indica (chulta)
Erythrina spp. (coral tree)
Eucalyptus spp. (gum tree)
Grevillea spp. (spider flower)
Halesia spp. (snowdrop tree)
Jacaranda mimosifolia
Laburnum x *watereri* 'Vossii'
Magnolia spp. and cvs.
Malus spp. and cvs. (crab apple)
Melia azedarach (bead tree)
Michelia doltsopa 'Silver Cloud'
Paulownia spp.
Prunus spp. (ornamental cherry)
Pyrus calleryana 'Bradford'
P. calleryana 'Chanticleer'
Sorbus spp. (mountain ash)
Staphylea holocarpa 'Rosea'
Stewartia spp.
Styrax spp. (snowbell)
Tabebuia spp.
Trachycarpus fortunei (Chusan palm)

Japanese flowering cherries, with their delicate pink and white single or double flowers, are among the most breathtaking of spring-flowering trees.

The early spring flowers of deciduous trees are more visible because there are no leaves to hide the flowers. Blooms can vary in size from the huge blooms of *Magnolia campbellii* (Campbell's magnolia), which can grow to 30cm (12in) across, to the clusters of dainty flowers of the *Prunus* cultivars (Japanese flowering cherries).

Conifers are wind pollinated and have no need for decorative flowers to attract pollinating insects, but many palm trees do have large clusters of flowers. Among the most attractive are those produced by *Trachycarpus fortunei* (Chusan palm) and its close relatives, which produce panicles, 60cm (24in) or more long, of hundreds of small yellow flowers.

Among the flowering evergreens are the forms of *Eucalyptus* spp. (gum tree), which feature small clusters of creamy-white, pink and occasionally red flowers.

The stunning array of trees that flower during the spring heralds the arrival of the new season in temperate zones. Spring is the most colourful of the seasons.

The giant blooms of *Magnolia campbellii* are a welcome sight in spring, and their true beauty is best revealed when they are viewed against a clear blue sky.

Crataegus laevigata 'Punicea', a hawthorn cultlivar, has stunning flowers.

Trees for summer flowers

Aesculus indica (Indian horse chestnut)
Banksia spp.
Barringtonia asiatica
Brownea macrophylla (Panama flame tree)
Calliandra spp. (powder puff tree)
Callistemon spp. (bottlebrush)
Calodendrum capense (Cape chestnut)
Catalpa bignonioides (Indian bean tree)
Catalpa fargesii (Chinese bean tree)
C. fargesii f. *duclouxii*
C. ovata (yellow catalpa)
C. x *erubescens* 'J.C. Teas' (syn. 'Hybrida')
Citrus spp.
Cladrastis kentukea (yellow wood)
C. kentukea 'Perkins Pink'
C. sinensis (Chinese yellow wood)
Cornus 'Porlock'
C. kousa (kousa dogwood)
C. Stellar hybrids
Crataegus spp.
Eucalyptus spp. (gum tree)
Lagerstroemia spp.
Magnolia grandiflora (bull bay magnolia)
M. oborata (Japanese big-leaf magnolia)
Metrosideros spp. (rata)
Robinia x *margaretta* 'Pink Cascade'
Robinia x *slavinii* 'Hillieri'
Stewartia spp.
Tabebuia spp.

Autumn colour

One of the most dramatic sights in our gardens, autumn colour occurs as the cool, lush foliage of summer gives way to autumnal tints that herald the arrival of winter.

Some species begin to change colour earlier than others, so that the period extends from summer to late autumn. For example, *Liquidambar styraciflua* (sweet gum) can begin to adopt its autumn hues in midsummer and still be producing stunning burgundy, red and yellow shades in mid-autumn, giving almost five months of interest.

The range and intensity of autumn colour can vary from year to year according to the amount of rainfall and what the summer temperatures were. They can also be affected by how quickly temperatures fall in early autumn, when the green pigment in the leaves (chlorophyll) breaks down to reveal the other pigments.

If a tree is under stress – if it is short of water or planted in nutrient-poor soil, for example – it will produce good autumn colour but the leaves will fall off quickly. If summer has been kind, with adequate rain, the pigments will break down slowly and the autumn colour will last much longer.

Another major influence on the autumn colour that a tree produces is soil pH. Many trees produce better autumn colour when they are grown in acidic soils than they do in alkaline soils, even if they can thrive in soils with a high pH.

Of the major species of tree that are planted for autumn colour, most will produce their best hues when they are grown in neutral to acidic soil. *Acer rubrum* (red maple), for example, will grow in slightly alkaline soil, but the autumn colour will be much more impressive when it is sited in acidic soil.

Acer japonicum (full moon maple) is a good small garden tree with vibrant autumn colour.

However, there are exceptions to the rule. *Parrota persica* (Persian ironwood) will produce vibrant autumn colour in alkaline soils.

The colourful autumn leaves brighten up the dullest day and provide a beautiful flourish before the trees shed their leaves and lie dormant until spring.

The white trunk of *Betula papyrifera* (paper birch) contrasts with the fiery autumn tints.

Taxodium distichum (swamp cypress) produces rich brown autumn tints as its fern-like green foliage changes in autumn. In winter, its silhouette is one of the most distinctive of all trees.

In larger gardens, trees with bold autumn tints can be planted to replicate the colours that are seen in natural woodlands. The aim should be to plant trees so that various tints are mixed together. In a small garden, however, combining autumn colours should be approached with caution, although the careful planting of shrubs and perennial grasses will enhance and complement the effect of the trees.

Trees for autumn colour

Acer buergerianum (trident maple)
A. campestre (field maple)
A. capillipes (snakebark maple)
A. cappadocicum (Cappadocian maple)
A. davidii (David's maple)
A. davidii 'Ernest Wilson'
A. davidii 'George Forrest'
A. davidii 'Madeline Spitta'
A. x *freemanii* 'Armstrong' (Freeman's maple)
A. x *freemanii* 'Autumn Blaze'
A. x *freemanii* 'Celebration'
A. x *freemanii* 'Morgan'
A. griseum (paperbark maple)
A. grosseri var. *hersii* (Hers's maple)
A. japonicum 'Aconitifolium' (full moon maple)
A. japonicum 'Vitifolium'
A. palmatum (Japanese maple)
A. platanoides 'Palmatifidum'
A. pycnanthum (Japanese red maple)
A. rubrum (red maple)
A. rubrum 'October Glory'
A. rubrum 'Schlesingeri'
A. rufinerve (red-vein maple)
A. saccharinum (silver maple)
A. saccharum (sugar maple)
A. sterculiaceum (Himalayan maple)
A. triflorum (three-flowered maple)
Carpinus betulus (common hornbeam)
C. caroliniana (American hornbeam)
Carya cordiformis (bitternut)
C. illinoinensis (pecan)
C. ovata (shagbark hickory)
Castanea dentata (American sweet chestnut)
C. sativa (sweet chestnut)
Cercidiphyllum japonicum (katsura tree)
Cladrastis kentukea (yellow wood)
Cornus florida (flowering dogwood)
C. 'Eddie's White Wonder'
Cotinus spp. (smoke tree)
Crataegus spp. (hawthorn)
Fagus grandifolia (American beech)
F. orientalis (oriental beech)
F. sylvatica (common beech)
Fraxinus americana 'Autumn Purple'
F. angustifolia 'Raywood' (claret ash)
F. ornus (manna ash)
Ginkgo biloba spp.
Koelreuteria paniculata (golden rain tree)
Lagerstroemia spp.
Liquidambar spp. (sweet gum)
Liriodendron spp. (tulip tree)
Malus spp. and cvs. (crab apple)
Metasequoia glyptostroboides (dawn redwood)
Nyssa sylvatica (tupelo)
Parrotia persica (Persian ironwood)
Prunus sargentii (Sargent cherry)
Pseudolarix amabilis (golden larch)
Pyrus calleryana 'Bradford'
P. calleryana 'Chanticleer'
Quercus spp. (oak, some)
Sassafras albidum
Stewartia spp.
Taxodium distichum (swamp cypress)
T. distichum var. *imbricatum* 'Nutans'
Ulmus spp. (elm)
Zelkova spp.

Autumn fruits and seeds

Trees produce their harvests of fruits and seeds in autumn. The range of shapes and colours is enormous, and includes vividly coloured holly berries, which are borne in abundance, as well as more intricate two-winged seeds that hang between the vibrant autumn leaves of *Acer palmatum* (Japanese maple).

Anyone wanting to extend the period of seasonal interest that is offered by trees should consider their potential for bearing fruits, berries and seeds, especially in a wildlife garden, where a succession of seeds and fruits can attract a diverse range of native and migratory birds.

The attractive bright red berries of the *Sorbus intermedia* (Swedish whitebeam), which is native to north-west Europe, appear in late summer.

Winter bark and stems

There are many trees with attractive stems and bark. Some have bark flakes that hang in ribbons from the trunk, while others have highly coloured bark or white stems that glisten in the winter sun.

Colourful winter stems and bark are most noticeable on deciduous trees once their foliage has fallen. Even on evergreen trees and conifers, the bark and stem patterns seem more pronounced in winter. Trees grown for their winter bark should be sited where they are backlit by the winter sun, so that they can be seen to best effect.

These highly ornamental trees are ideal as focal points or lawn specimens, as well as welcome additions to mixed borders. Space permitting, they even make spectacular avenues. The stark white stems of a *Eucalyptus* would create a beautiful avenue in a large garden, while *Acer griseum* (paperbark maple), with its flaking, cinnamon-coloured bark, would look stunning in a smaller-scale design.

Most pines produce woody female cones that protect the seeds.

Trees for autumn fruits and seeds

Abies spp. (fir)
Acer pseudoplatanus f. *erythrocarpum*
Artocarpus altilis (breadfruit)
Bauhinia spp. (mountain ebony)
Calodendron capense (Cape chestnut)
Calophyllum inophyllum (Alexandrian laurel)
Carya cordiformis (bitternut)
C. illinoinensis (pecan)
C. ovata (shagbark hickory)
Castanea spp. (sweet chestnut)
Catalpa bignonioides (Indian bean tree)
Cercis canadensis (eastern redbud)
C. siliquastrum (Judas tree)
Clusia major (autograph tree)
Cornus spp. (dogwood)
Corylus colurna (Turkish hazel)
Crataegus spp. (hawthorn)
Davidia involucrata (handkerchief tree)
Dillenia indica (chulta)
Elaeocarpus angustifolius (blue quandong)
Ilex spp. (holly)
Juglans regia (common walnut)
Koelreuteria paniculata spp.
Magnolia spp. and cvs.
Malus spp. and cvs. (crab apple)
Melia azedarach 'Jade Snowflake'
Morus spp. (mulberry)
Olea europaea (European olive)
Picea spp. (spruce)
Pinus spp. (pines)
Platanus spp. (plane)
Pterocarya stenoptera (wing nut)
Sorbus spp. (mountain ash)

Trees for colourful bark and stems

Acer capillipes (snakebark maple)
A. x *conspicuum* cvs.
A. davidii cvs.
A. 'Gingerbread'
A. griseum (paperbark maple)
A. grosseri var. *hersii* (Hers's maple)
A. negundo 'Winter Lightning'
A. palmatum 'Sango-kaku' (coral bark maple)
A. pensylvanicum (moosewood)
A. rufinerve spp.
A. 'White Tigress'
Betula albosinensis (Chinese red birch)
B. ermanii (Erman's birch)
B. nigra (black birch)
B. pendula (silver birch)
B. utilis var. *jacquemontii* (Himalayan birch)
Eucalyptus spp. (gum tree)
Lagerstroemia spp.
Metasequoia glyptostroboides (dawn redwood)
Parrotia persica (Persian ironwood)
Pinus bungeana (lacebark pine)
P. densiflora (Japanese red pine)
P. sylvestris (Scots pine)
Platanus spp. (plane)
Prunus maackii (Manchurian cherry)
P. serrula (Tibetan cherry)
Salix spp. (willow)
Stewartia spp.
Ulmus spp. (elm)

Although the young bark of *Betula nigra* 'Heritage' (black birch) is smoooth, creamy and orange, the older bark is corrugated.

Winter flowers and habit

A number of trees flower in winter. Many are highly scented because the trees have to work hard to attract the few potential pollinators that are around during the cold months. The delicate blooms can be easily damaged by freezing temperatures, chilling winds and snow, so the ephemeral beauty of these flowers is especially welcome. Winter-flowering trees are best used as lawn specimens or sited where they may be easily seen from a window or near a path, so their scent can be appreciated.

A garden in a temperate area in winter takes on a very different atmosphere from that which it has during other seasons, as it is reduced to its barest essentials. Although a tree may not possess attractive flowers or bark, its silhouette against the winter sky can be as striking as any array of blooms or coloured stems. It is while the trees are bereft of their leaves that we can appreciate their shape, and it is during this time that the outlines of trees with weeping and columnar habits, or with ghostly bark such as the silver birches, are most clearly seen, looking as beautiful as the most intricate sculpture.

Tecoma stans (yellow elder) is a beautiful winter flowering tree for tropical climates, but can also be grown as a container-grown tree in a conservatory or glasshouse.

Trees for winter flowers and habit

Flowers (F) or habit (H):
Acer campestre 'Evelyn' (H)
A. x *freemanii* 'Celebration' (H)
A. rubrum 'Armstrong' (H)
A. saccharum 'Arrowhead' (H)
A. saccharum subsp. *nigrum* 'Monumentale' (H)
Acacia dealbata (F)
Calodendron capense (F)
Cornus controversa (table dogwood) (H)
C. mas (cornelian cherry) (F)
Corylus colurna (Turkish hazel) (H)
Eriobotrya (loquat) (F)
Parrotia persica (Persian ironwood) (F)
Tecoma stans (yellow elder) (F)

Buying trees

Once you have decided upon a tree, you need to ensure that the one you buy is strong, healthy and the right size. There are two main outlets for purchasing trees – a nursery or a garden centre. However, the internet is fast becoming an outlet for more exotic trees.

Specialist nurseries carry a wide range of trees and shrubs. Many have a mail-order service, which can be invaluable if the nursery is not easy for you to reach.

Tree nurseries

When buying a tree, specialized tree nurseries are a good option, as the staff should be able to give you up-to-date information on the best trees for your garden. Some nurseries open only at limited times, so check before you visit.

Many nurseries specialize in different growing techniques and offer large, container-grown plants for people who want an instant effect. Others sell only bare-root or rootballed plants in winter and spring. If you can, visit more than one nursery so you can compare the plants that are available. The smaller nurseries usually offer modest quantities of a limited number of tree species – and then only to personal callers. Others have a mail-order service, but only send out plants at limited times of the year.

Garden centres

General plant nurseries and garden centres usually carry a wide range of container-grown trees throughout the year and at certain times in winter. Also, a few of the larger outlets stock bare-root and rootballed specimens. The most commonly grown trees will usually be available at these outlets, and from time to time you might find some slightly more unusual trees.

Large DIY stores are offering an increasingly wide range of trees, although these are mostly container-grown specimens. Although they are often inexpensive, unfortunately, they are frequently poorly cared for, so look at potential 'bargains' carefully before you commit yourself.

Bare-rooted trees are sold with their roots exposed after most of the soil has been removed and their roots trimmed. These trees need to be planted immediately after purchase.

Internet and mail order

Mail order and the internet offer much wider selections of trees than those available from a single supplier and many of the larger nurseries now also offer online searching and purchase. The disadvantages are that you do not see the plants before they arrive; there is always a risk that the tree may be damaged in transit; and with a bare-rooted specimen you must be ready to plant the tree as soon as it is delivered, which may not always be convenient.

What to buy

Trees are available in different sizes and forms. Large trees provide instant effect, but small ones establish much more easily and may even overtake a larger (and more expensive) specimen planted at the same time. If you want to plant at any time during the year (except when the ground is frozen or waterlogged), container-grown trees are the best option. If you wish to plant in winter, bare-rooted or rootballed (balled and burlapped) plants are worth considering.

Container-grown trees

Trees that are grown in plastic pots, wooden boxes or some other type of container should have been regularly potted on so that their root systems have been able to develop freely. Container-grown plants are not usually affected by transplanting as they have well-established root systems, which are only slightly disrupted during planting.

Container-grown trees can be planted at any time of the year, except when the ground is frozen or waterlogged. Periods of drought are also best avoided unless you are prepared to undertake the necessary watering. If they have to be kept for a while before you have time to plant, store them in a shady, sheltered place and water regularly.

Container-grown trees tend to be more expensive than bare-root or rootballed trees, and the restriction on the size of the pot required for a large tree is a major disadvantage.

Rootballed trees

You can buy deciduous trees more than 4m (12ft) high, palms over 1.5m (5ft) and many evergreens, including conifers, in this form, and they are usually less expensive than container-grown trees. The plants are grown in nursery beds and are lifted in winter. The whole root system is wrapped in netting, hessian (burlap) or a similar material. When you are moving a rootballed plant, you should carry it by holding the rootball. Before planting, make sure that all the wrapping material around the rootball has been removed.

Although a rootballed plant can be stored for a while before planting, if necessary, it is best planted as soon after purchase as possible because the root system will have been disturbed when it was taken from the nursery bed.

If the plant has to be stored for any period of time, place it in a shady position, water the rootball if it looks dry and apply a mulch, such as composted bark, to prevent it from drying out. Rootballed trees should be planted between midwinter and early spring.

Bare-root trees

As their name suggests, bare-root trees have no soil around the roots when they are sold, which is during the trees' dormant period in winter. The only trees that can be sold as bare-rooted specimens are deciduous trees that are dormant and leafless when lifted.

Bare-rooted trees are the cheapest and most portable of all the types of tree available for purchase, but the range of varieties is usually more limited. They are grown in a nursery bed, and each year they are undercut, which involves pruning the main roots to encourage the tree to develop a vigorous, branching root system.

When the tree is ready for sale, it is lifted and the roots are again trimmed. At this time, all or most of the soil is removed from around the roots, so the tree should be planted as soon after purchase as possible.

If the plant has to be stored the root system should be covered with damp compost (soil mix) or bark chippings or it should be heeled in (planted leaning at an angle) in another part of the garden until you are ready to plant it properly in the site you have chosen.

Bare-rooted plants need planting immediately after you buy them so that the roots do not dry out or become damaged.

After being lifted at the nursery, rootballed trees are sold with their root system wrapped in netting or hessian (burlap).

Choosing a healthy tree

Once you have decided on the type of tree you want, you need to make sure you acquire a healthy specimen. As well as the obvious benefits, there is always a risk of introducing pests and diseases into your garden with a new tree, especially if it is in a container.

Buying trees

Specialist nurseries offer the widest choice of trees for sale, but you should visit nurseries or garden centres to see if the plants look well cared for, as well as asking other gardeners which suppliers they recommend.

When you are selecting a garden tree, there are three areas to which you should pay particular attention: the root system, the trunk and the branches and leaves.

Roots

A well-developed and healthy root system is essential if a tree is to become successfully established in your garden, so when you are selecting a new tree the first task is to check the roots. Avoid plants with roots that emerge from the soil at peculiar angles or that seem to be strangling or cutting across the trunk. This is especially important if the tree is container-grown or rootballed.

If a container-grown tree has been allowed to grow for too long in a pot that is too small, it will be pot-bound and the roots will be tightly wound around the sides of the pot. When you plant the tree, the roots won't grow out into the surrounding soil, causing the tree to be unstable, nor will the roots extend into the soil in search of nutrients.

Although container-grown trees are more expensive, they are easier to handle as they can be planted when you are ready.

This *Acer griseum* has a sound trunk and straight growth. These are qualities that you should look for when buying a tree.

Another indication that a tree is pot-bound is if there are roots protruding through the drainage holes. Even worse, the tree may have rooted itself into the ground beneath the pot. Avoid plants where you can see that large roots have been cut off close to the drainage holes.

Misshapen plastic pots, distorted by the roots exerting pressure on the sides as they have developed, are another sign of neglect. Avoid container-grown plants with weeds on the surface of the soil, as this suggests that the plants have been neglected. Weeds not only compete for nutrients but can also be hosts for pests and diseases.

Sometimes roots grow too close to the trunk and circle the base of a tree at or just below the surface. As the trunk increases in girth, so does the root, and as both grow they exert pressure on each other, sometimes causing the trunk to grow abnormally or, even worse, to fail at this point. This is known as girdling.

Trunks

There should be a clear taper along the trunk, with a distinct flail or flare at the base where it meets the ground. Trees naturally develop reaction or reinforced timber at points where they move or bear extra weight.

When a trunk constantly sways in the wind, the movement is transferred down the trunk to the point where it cannot move – that is, where it joins the root system. This pressure is distributed along the lower one-third of the trunk, preventing it from cracking or breaking. This point is reinforced with additional wood fibre, which is why it is thicker.

When you are selecting a tree, check the trunk for defects, such as linear cracks, which may lead to structural damage or even trunk failure. There should be no damaged or dead sections of bark, caused during lifting, transplanting or growing, because they can lead to stem or trunk rot which will affect the structural integrity of the trunk.

This stunning *Acer japonicum* 'Vitifolium' is a good example of healthy tree, with well-spaced branches, a straight trunk, and good leaf colour.

Branches and leaves

The last areas to inspect are the branches and leaves. The branches should be well spaced along the trunk, and there should be no damaged, dead or crossing branches. Smaller branches may cross within the crown, but any larger ones should have been removed by the nursery to allow the crown to develop with an open and balanced array of branches.

Check to see how recently removed branches have been pruned – cuts that have been made too close to the trunk may allow a disease to penetrate the tree's natural defences, causing serious problems. Look at the bark on the branches to check that there are no splits and cracks.

Make sure that the leaves and shoots are completely free from pests and diseases. Check, too, that the leaves are the appropriate colour for the tree. They should not be too yellow or otherwise discoloured, nor should there be patches of yellow between the veins, as this is a symptom of nutrient deficiency. If you are specifically buying a tree for an unusual leaf colour or variegation, make sure that all the leaves are coloured and show no signs of reversion.

Finally, look at the extension growth of the stem, which is a good indicator of the level and consistency of a tree's vegetative growth from year to year. Each tree produces new shoots, which will grow throughout the summer until autumn, when the growth is stopped by falling temperatures and lower light levels. When new growth begins the following year, a scar appears, indicating the end of the previous year's growth and the beginning of the current year's growth.

If a tree has been well cared for at the nursery and consistently had sufficient nutrients, water and sunlight, the extension or vegetative growth should be similar from year to year. If the tree has been subjected to any setbacks during a year, the vegetative growth will be shorter.

Check for healthy leaves before you buy your tree. This *Eucryphia glutinosa* has rich, natural-coloured and pest-free leaves.

Tree gardening techniques

Trees can be used in myriad ways in the garden, not only to create attractive landscapes, but also to produce fruit, block out noise, frame a view or provide a focal point. Whatever the purpose of the tree, it is crucial that you fully understand how to nurture and care for garden trees. This understanding must start from the ground itself – with a knowledge of how to prepare the earth and provide a nutrient bed in which to plant the young tree – and work up to pruning and training, so that you can manipulate the habit of your trees.

If things go wrong, however, you may also need to know how to transplant a tree and re-establish it in a new location.

The careful choosing, siting and nurturing of trees can produce the most stunning effects in the garden.

Different soils

There are are several different types of soil, which are distinguished by the basic particles they contain, such as sand, clay, silt and composted organic material. In addition, the soil is colonized by earthworms and other soil-dwelling organisms that help break down nutrients and make them available to plants. This, too, alters the nature of the soil.

Sandy soils

Free-draining sandy soils tend to warm up quickly in spring, so plants get away to an early start. However, they also cool down quickly in winter. The proportion of sand compared to other particles determines just how freely the soil drains, and these soils can also vary according to the proportion of silica or quartz particles they contain.

Sandy soils may be either acidic or alkaline. Soils that were once part of the seabed may, for example, contain a high proportion of shells, which are made up of calcium, and so they will be alkaline. A sandy soil that has evolved over time and has been exposed to high rainfall, cool temperatures and slowly decomposing conifer needles will be acidic.

Because it is free-draining, nutrients are quickly washed through this type of soil. It can be worked at any time of the year, but it requires close attention in spring and summer, when it can dry out quickly.

Digging in plenty of organic matter will improve its ability to retain both moisture and nutrients. Mulching with organic material, such as garden compost, bark chippings, rotted manure, mushroom compost or leaf mould, will help to conserve moisture in the soil and reduce the chance of weeds germinating and competing for nutrients. More importantly, it will also add valuable nutrients to the soil. For this reason, it is essential to mulch free-draining soils annually.

Sandy loams

A soil that is described as 'sandy loam' is one of the best types to have. The soil consists of a blend of sand, clay and silt particles, with the sand being present in the highest proportion. These soils are not only free-draining and moisture-retentive but also rich in nutrients.

They are easy to work at any time of the year and warm up quickly in spring but cool at a more even rate in autumn. They tend to be less hungry than sandy soils and require less frequent irrigation and the addition of less organic matter.

Clay soils

Although they are the most difficult to cultivate, once clay soils are successfully worked they are among the most fertile because clay particles are able to attract and hold nutrients in a form that makes them readily available to plants.

Clay particles bond together tightly, so when this type of soil is wet it can be difficult to dig. Moreover, the surface of the soil may compact and cause puddling. As it dries, large cracks can appear in the soil, while the surface forms an impermeable layer from which water simply runs into the cracks and is quickly carried away.

Testing soil

Finding out what type of soil you have is easy and does not require any specialist equipment. This test is ultimately a matter of judgement and will only give you a relative picture of the sort of soil you have. However, it is surprisingly accurate. Simply take a small amount of soil – about a teaspoonful will do – in the palm of your hand. Moisten with a little water (not too much but enough to make it just workable). Once moistened, try to form the soil into one of the shapes shown above.

1 Begin by forming a ball. If it stays together, then proceed to the next shape. If it does not form a ball, then you have a sandy soil.

2 If you can flatten the ball without it breaking up, then you have a silty sand or a loamy sand.

3 If you can roll the flattened ball into a thick sausage shape, then you have a loam.

4 A soil that can be rolled into a thin 'sausage' is a clay loam.

5 If you can bend the soil into a ring shape, then you have a clay soil.

Clay soils retain water, which makes them slow to warm up in spring but slow to cool down in autumn and winter. Adding large quantities of horticultural sand will improve the drainage, although if puddling persists it might be necessary to investigate underlying problems and even install a drainage system.

When a new tree is planted into poorly drained clay soil it can be set slightly proud of the surrounding level to allow it to establish before its roots grow into the wider soil. Remember that planting proud will make the roots dry out more easily in periods of drought.

Digging over clay soils in autumn allows winter frosts to weather the particles and this helps to unbind the clay. Organic matter can be more easily incorporated in spring, when the soil is more workable. You can also add it as a mulch, allowing earthworms to take it down into the soil. Adding garden lime in autumn or spring can help to unbind the particles and open up the soil, although adding large quantities of lime will raise the pH if it is applied annually and over many years. Garden lime is highly soluble and will cause nutrient deficiencies in lime-hating plants.

Peaty soils

Depending on how they were formed, peaty soils can be highly acidic or neutral. Upland peat is formed by the decay of mosses and other plant material over a long period to form a dense layer of acidic organic matter.

Lowland or marsh peat results when flooded areas of marsh slowly decompose over a long period of time. Areas of natural peat are often exposed and have high annual rainfall, even flooding for part of the year.

PREPARING THE GROUND FOR PLANTING TREES

1 Organic material such as well-rotted garden compost or farmyard manure is high in nutrients. Fork in when the soil is dug. For heavy soils this is best done in the autumn.

2 If the soil has already been dug, the organic material can be lightly forked in or left on the surface. The worms will complete the task of working it into the soil.

Trees that occur naturally on peat soils are able to deal with the high quantities of some nutrients, like iron, as well as deficiencies of other minerals. Peat soils, found in most gardens, develop in areas that were once coniferous forests and that have high annual rainfall. Over thousands of years, the needles from the coniferous trees decomposed to form a peaty layer on the soil surface. This layer, which can be quite deep, is rich in humus and is moisture-retentive – ideal conditions for trees.

Peat soils are often slow to warm up in spring but cool down quickly in autumn, while the drainage will depend on the nature of the subsoil. A much wider range of plants can be grown in peaty soils than in chalk.

Chalk soils

Often free-draining, open and quite shallow, chalk, or calcareous, soils are one of the most difficult types to cultivate. Because the chalk keeps the soil open, they are, like sandy soils, hungry. The clay or silt particles they contain can cause them to bind during wet weather, but although the surface of the soil may compact when it is wet, it seldom cracks when dry.

The shallow nature of chalk soil will inhibit the depth to which the root system of trees can spread, so the roots of trees in chalk soil may be much shallower and less extensive than those growing in deeper soil. This may cause young trees to become unstable in strong winds, and they will often be prone to drought.

Chalk soils have a high pH, which will limit the range of plants that can be grown because lime will lock up other nutrients and cause poor growth and yellowing of the leaves. Such soils require an annual application of bulky, well-rotted farm manure, deep mulching and occasional irrigation.

Understanding soil

Of all the factors that influence the way garden trees grow, the most important is the soil. Its make-up and pH (acidity or alkalinity) may result in not just poor growth but even the death of a newly planted tree – but get it right and your tree will thrive.

Reducing soil acidity

The acidity of your soil can be reduced by adding lime some weeks before planting. First, check the soil with a soil-testing kit to see how much lime is required.

Topsoil

Most gardeners are concerned with the top layer of soil – the topsoil. This is a comparatively shallow zone that contains oxygen, nutrients and moisture in forms that the tree roots can use. This area can vary greatly in depth, although 25–30cm (10–12in) is normal.

However, in shallow soils over chalk or rock and in tropical forests, the layer may be as little as 10cm (4in) deep, whereas at the base of valleys, in river basins and in areas that have been cultivated for a long time, topsoils can be much deeper – as much as 1–2m (3–6ft) deep or more.

Subsoil

The layer of soil below the topsoil is known as subsoil, which can vary greatly in character. It can be very stony or formed of chalk or clay and the composition will influence the way the topsoil drains.

Subsoil can be easily identified because it is a different colour from the topsoil. It is deficient in the beneficial oxygen, humus and micro-organisms that are found in topsoil, although it can be cultivated into a workable medium that will eventually become topsoil.

If the subsoil is of reasonable quality, tree roots will grow into it for improved anchorage. Some new housing complexes are developed on sites where the existing topsoil has been removed, leaving only the subsoil.

On completing the buildings, the contractors often return a shallow layer of topsoil and then turf the gardens. In such areas the soil will require considerable work to improve its aeration and humus content.

CHECKING PH LEVELS

Soil-testing kits of various degrees of sophistication are widely available, such as this electronic meter, which tests the pH level.

THE STRUCTURE OF THE SOIL

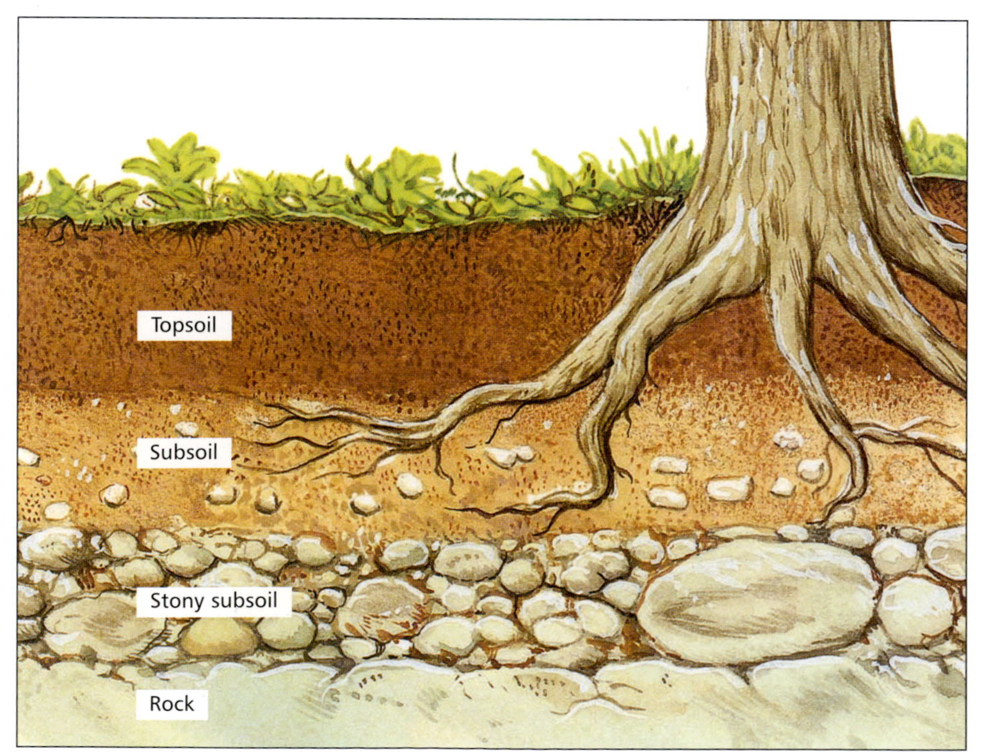

Soil pH

Perhaps the most important aspect of soil is its pH. This is the measure of a soil's acidity or alkalinity, and it will determine the plants you can grow in your garden.

A soil's pH is measured on a scale from 1 to 14. Soils with a pH below 7 are acidic (ericaceous); soils with a pH above 7 are alkaline. Plants that have adapted to growing on acidic soil are known as calcifuges and plants that have adapted to soil with a high pH (alkaline) are calcicoles, which means they are acid-hating or lime-loving plants.

The availability or otherwise of minerals in the soil affects a plant's growth. On soils with a pH below 4.5, nutrients such as aluminium, iron and manganese are so readily available that they become toxic to certain plants. However, other mineral elements, including nitrogen, phosphorus, potassium, calcium and magnesium, are locked up and plants suffer from mineral deficiencies.

In low pH soils the activity and effectiveness of fungi and bacteria, which normally help break down organic matter, are greatly reduced, as is the activity of earthworms. When the pH is above 7, deficiencies of manganese and iron are likely to occur, while lime is freely available.

The best pH for most trees is between 5.5 and 7.5, when essential nutrients are readily available and earthworms and other beneficial organisms can survive.

Planting an acid-loving tree in chalky soil quickly causes its leaves to turn yellow, stunts its growth, and the tree might eventually die, because the green pigment in the leaves begins to die and the tree cannot function.

Soil-testing kits

Cheap and reliable soil-testing kits are available from garden retailers that will indicate the nutrient balance in your soil and its pH level. For this to be of value you must test a representative sample of soil.

The most reliable way of doing this is to lay four canes on the soil surface in a large W shape, then use a trowel to dig a small hole, 15cm (6in) deep, at each point of the W, making a total of five holes. Scoop out some soil from each hole and place it in a garden sieve over a bucket. Mix the soil from the different holes before testing.

Make sure you do not test the soil where a compost heap has been, or where you have added a fertilizer, since this will not give you a true result for the garden as a whole.

TESTING YOUR SOIL FOR ITS NUTRIENT VALUES

1 Collect a soil sample from 10cm (4in) below the surface. Take several different samples and mix together for a representative test.

2 Follow the instructions on the kit. Usually, you mix 1 part soil with 5 parts distilled water. Shake well and then allow the water to settle.

3 Using the pipette provided with the kit, draw off some of the liquid from the top of the jar.

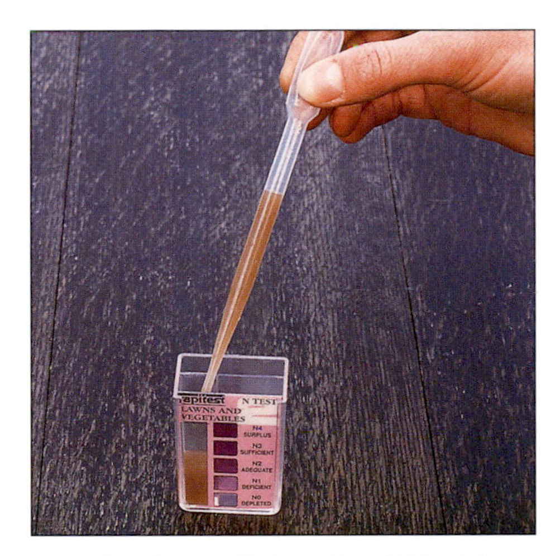

4 Having drawn off about 5cm (2in) of the solution, transfer the sample to the test chamber in the plastic container.

5 Select a colour-coded capsule (one for each nutrient). Put in the chamber, replace the cap and shake well. The result will appear.

6 After a few minutes, you can compare the colour of the liquid with the shade panel shown on the side of the container.

Beneficial soil organisms for trees

In recent years we have become more aware that many of our garden trees grow in a stressful environment where they do not have the benefit of the soil-borne fungi and bacteria that are found in their natural ecosystems. Without these elements, which help trees absorb nutrients, it is harder for them to flourish.

Fighting deficiencies

To combat this deficit in the somewhat sterile conditions of our garden soils, where little nutrient recycling takes place, mycorrhizal fungi or biostimulants can be incorporated into a tree planting pit or applied to an ailing mature tree. This will dramatically increase nutrient and water uptake and improve the overall well-being of the tree.

It is often recommended that one or the other system is adopted, but often they complement each other.

Today many such products are available from a variety of outlets, making them widely available to the amateur gardener, so check on the packaging to find out which one is suitable for your tree.

Mycorrhizal fungi

Widespread in natural habitats such as forests and woodlands, mycorrhizal fungi have a symbiotic relationship with the root systems of trees. They colonize the roots and greatly increase the area that the trees' roots are able to cover, and so assist with and increase the uptake of water and nutrients.

Various different species of mycorrhizal fungi exist and certain trees have developed particular relationships with specific fungi: some are only found on conifers; others are only found on deciduous trees; and some groups are specifically associated with certain habitats, or a certain tree species.

However, recent studies have proved that the percentage of mycorrhizal fungi found in garden borders, lawns and in urban settings is considerably less than the quantity that is found in a native meadow, woodland or forest. This is mainly because there is far less nutrient recycling in gardens due to our constant urge to clean dead and dying material away, rather than let it break down naturally.

Bay boletus are found only under conifers.

The brown birch bolete thrives under birches.

Mycorrhizal fungi groups

Mycorrhizal fungi can be broken down into two specific groups. One colonizes the outside of tree roots and is called ectomycorrhizae, and is generally associated with the roots of conifers and hardwoods, such as *Fagus*, *Betula* and *Quercus*.

The second grows into the cells of the root system and is called endomycorrhizae. These are often found on hardwood trees, fruit and nut trees and shrubs. However, due to the relationships between different types of trees, most mycorrhizal fungi mixes contain both types with a broad spectrum mix, as those fungi unable to colonize will perish.

Benefits to trees

Mycorrhizal fungi can improve the overall health of trees, and so make them more drought- and disease-resistant, which in turn can make them more adaptable to a wide range of garden habitats.

The benefits of mycorrhizal treatments can increase the total surface area of root systems by as much as 700 per cent. Due to the increase in volume, they can occupy more than a hundred times more soil than a non-mycorrhizal-inoculated tree root system. They can grow through the soil up to 6m (20ft), radiating away from a host tree, and help the tree to become more resistant to many root diseases caused by soil-borne fungi and pests.

These safe and simple to use inoculants are now widely available from garden centres and over the internet. They can be added to a planting pit and lightly forked in to the soil. However, conditions must be right for their colonization: the soil must be moist and warm enough and the fungi should be in direct contact with the roots.

In a woodland setting there is a constant supply of organic matter being broken down by a wide range of organisms. This organic matter in turn provides nutrients for the plants and trees that grow there, enabling them to flourish and proliferate in great numbers.

Biostimulants

The term biostimulant is used to describe various natural products that can be applied in a similar manner to a fertilizer, and that will have a positive effect on the vigour or health of a tree. Biostimulants are enzymes and essential elements that occur naturally in the soil. They can also be added to the soil to increase the number of friendly soil-borne bacteria and fungi.

During periods when trees are under stress, vital elements are used to protect the tree. However, if they become deficient in the soil or the root system has insufficient energy to absorb them, the tree's health may decline and allow disease to spread.

When this occurs, the tree or its roots will not produce enough vitamins, amino acids or hormones to recover from such stress. However, adding biostimulants can help the tree recover by enhancing food production and increasing the efficiency of the leaves to trap sunlight, so increasing the production of simple sugars. They also increase antioxidants, nutrient availability and the water-holding capacity of the soil.

Another major benefit of biostimulants is that they can increase the quantity of humus in the soil. Humus is made up of decomposed organic matter that builds up in the soil over time, and which improves moisture and nutrient retention.

Biostimulants also increase the availability of two important micronutrients, phosphate and potash, while stabilizing nutrient uptake in high pH or very salty soils. Also, because biostimulants increase the efficiency of nutrient uptake, less fertilizer is needed.

A variety of mycorrhizal fungi and biostimulant products is available and these can be applied directly into the soil during planting, or watered in, or in the case of biostimulants applied as a soil drench or foliar feed.

Biostimulants can be watered in to the soil.

Planting a tree

After choosing and buying a tree that is suitable for your garden, the next important step is to plant it so that it becomes successfully established. Of all the causes of death associated with newly planted trees, the most common is planting too deeply, which suffocates the trunk and causes it to rot. However, if you observe a few simple guidelines, tree planting is relatively easy.

Digging the hole

A common mistake is to assume that a tree will require a deep, wide hole, filled with organic matter, growth regulators and improved soil. However, although soil improvers may be needed in a few situations, they are not usually necessary because it is far better to allow the tree to acclimatize to the soil in which it will spend the rest of its life rather than having to mollycoddle it for the rest of your life.

If possible, prepare the hole six to eight weeks before planting to allow the soil to settle, which will stop the tree from settling deeply. If the hole can be dug in autumn, when the soil is usually drier and more workable, so much the better because it will make the planting process easier and will reduce the risk of smearing the sides of the hole in heavy clay or silt soils. It will also minimize the risk of compacting the soil by standing on it or moving equipment around when it is wet.

If the tree is to be grown as a lawn specimen, then cut the turf to leave a square or circle of exposed soil between one and a half and two times the diameter of the container or rootball. For all other planting, dig a hole that is slightly deeper than the root system of the tree, but that is three times wider than the container or the rootball. If you are unsure of the size of the tree dig a square hole 1.2m x 1.2m (4ft x 4ft) and 30cm (12in) deep. Remove any perennial weeds and large stones and fork over the base. Fill the hole again and allow the area to settle.

When you have your tree, dig a hole slightly wider than the container or rootball and lightly fork the bottom. It is essential that the tree is planted so that it is the same level as it was originally, no matter how it was supplied. Lay a piece of timber or a cane across the hole so that you can check that it lines up with the nursery mark or dark stain at the base of the trunk, just above the point where the roots flare out from the trunk. If this mark is not clear, plant the tree slightly proud.

Placing mulch at the base of the newly planted tree will not only help to preserve the moisture in the soil but also help to prevent weed seeds from germinating.

PREPARATION PRIOR TO PLANTING

1 Prepare a circular or square area wider than the tree's rootball you are intending to plant.

2 After digging through the area, break any large lumps of soil with a folk, and remove any weeds.

3 Ensure that the hole is deep and wide enough to accomodate the tree's roots.

4 Add grit or sand on heavy soils, or organic matter on light soils. Allow to settle prior to planting.

HOW TO PLANT

1 Remove the tree from its wrapping or pot and place in the centre of the hole.

2 Begin to backfill around the tree with the excavated soil, using a spade.

3 Insert a stake to one side of the main stem, taking care not to damage the roots.

4 Tie the stem loosely to the cane with soft string or rubber tree ties.

5 Firm the tree in well with your hands or feet, without over compacting the soil.

6 Water the tree well after planting to help it to become established.

7 Mulch with straw to conserve moisture in the soil.

How to plant the tree

If the tree is in a container, remove the pot and use your fingers or a hand fork to carefully prise away some of the roots. Remove the sacking (burlap) from rootballed plants just before planting and tease out some of the roots. If you notice any damaged roots on a bare-rooted tree cut them away.

Set the tree in the hole and check the depth again, adding or removing soil if necessary. If you wish to, you can add biostimulants or mycorrhizal fungi to improve the tree's uptake of nutrients and water (see pages 72–3).

Begin to refill the hole, making sure that the soil is worked well between the roots. This is especially important for bare-rooted trees. Use your fingers or the heel of your shoe to make sure that there is maximum contact around the base of the tree and around the edge of the root zones, but be careful not to overcompact the soil. Refill in layers, firming as you go, until the tree is planted.

Water well and stake (see pages 80–5). To ensure that the tree gets off to the best possible start install a mulch mat and mulch around the tree (see pages 86–7).

Planting trees in containers

Some species can be successfully grown in containers. This allows us to grow trees that are unsuitable for our gardens' soil, that are not hardy and need protection, or that we want to move around to create flexibility in our gardens' design.

The advantage of pots

Using a container is one way of growing trees in locations where there is not a sufficient depth of soil for them to thrive, as with roof gardens. It is also possible to position trees in containers close to house walls without risking damaging the foundations.

Species that do not suit the type of soil in the wider garden can be grown in pots filled with acidic (ericaceous) or alkaline compost (soil mix), and it is also possible to choose comparatively tender species that would not survive outdoors in winter but that, when grown in a container, can be moved to the shelter of a greenhouse or conservatory during the coldest weather.

As long as they have been container-grown from the start, many tree species can be successfully grown in containers, where they can be kept smaller and more compact than similar species grown in the garden. Ideal species include palms, *Acer japonicum* and *A. palmatum* (Japanese maple), *Taxus* (yew), *Ilex* (holly) and many types of fruit tree, including apples, pears, oranges, loquats and olives.

In most cases, growing a tree in a container will restrict its ultimate size, but eventually, over time, many species will become too large and top-heavy, and it may be necessary to install an anchor system to secure the tree or its container to the ground to keep them stable.

Trees that are grown in containers have the same requirements as those that are grown in the open garden, but pruning, fertilizing and watering are even more important. Whenever you choose a container, you should remember that the weight and size of the tree and its container may make repotting the tree or replacing all the compost difficult or, in some cases, impossible.

Position is less of an issue with trees in containers because the tree can be moved, although the weight of the tree and a soil-filled container may mean that special equipment or extra help is necessary.

Japanese maples are widely grown in containers because their graceful habit, attractive foliage, and ease of pruning make them easy to cultivate.

Types of container

A tree requires the largest possible container to accommodate the rootball and soil. Trees above 3m (10ft) in height can become unstable, and evergreens, including conifers and palms, are most likely to be blown over because they retain

PLANTING A TREE IN A POT

1 Layer the pot with broken crocks or stones to help drainage and top with a layer of grit or vermiculite.

2 Begin to fill the pot with compost (soil mix). Add compost until the container is about a third full.

3 Remove the tree from the pot and gently tease out the roots, using a garden fork or your fingers.

their foliage throughout the year. Broad-based containers, such as half-tubs, tend to be more stable than narrow-based containers shaped like traditional plant pots.

Terracotta pots are widely available in a multitude of sizes and styles and at a wide range of prices, although larger, frost-resistant pots are expensive. They are available in traditional shapes, sometimes ornately patterned, or as straight-sided square or rectangular pots, which are more stable. Terracotta is attractive and suits most gardens.

When filled with moist soil terracotta pots are heavy, and they will break easily if blown over or if the tree roots exert too much pressure on the sides. Water evaporates more quickly from terracotta, so it is important to water regularly, sometimes every day, in sunny or windy weather. In areas with hard water, terracotta eventually becomes discoloured by lime scale.

Plastic containers have the advantages of being cheap and available in a range of colours, styles and sizes. They are lighter than terracotta pots and are a better choice if you want to move the tree around.

4 Place in the centre of the pot and fill with compost to about 2.5cm (1in) from the top to allow for watering.

Plastic containers are less likely than terracotta ones to be damaged if they fall over. Water does not evaporate through plastic, but because the material is thinner the roots within the container are more susceptible to changes in temperature, and the rootball may suffer not only from cold in winter but from overheating in summer.

Inexpensive plastic fades in strong sun, so the pots may not look as attractive, and they may become brittle, causing problems if you try to move the tree. Even expensive plastics will become discoloured in time.

Wooden and metal containers are both available, and both materials are more stable and robust than terracotta and plastic and are less likely to split or fall over. However, even treated wood will rot over time, and for this reason wooden tubs often have liners, and metal containers may rust.

The weight of both types means that they are difficult to move, and they are best kept for trees in permanent positions. It is essential that there are drainage holes in the base of the container, no matter what it is made from.

5 Water in well and, if you like, top-dress with grit to help retain moisture and make the pot look smart.

Aftercare

Every year in early spring remove the top 5–10cm (2–4in) of compost (taking care not to damage surface roots), replace it with fresh compost and water thoroughly. You should then add a slow-release fertilizer to the fresh compost to help replenish any lost or deficient nutrients.

A tree that has been in the same container for several years will become pot-bound and the roots will occupy most of the available space. When this happens the roots quickly take up water, and the tree is more prone to drying out and needs regular and thorough watering.

In hot weather it may be necessary to water several times a day to get sufficient water into the root zone. If possible, use collected rainwater, especially for ericaceous species, rather than domestic water. No matter how carefully you choose the species and containers, trees will eventually outgrow the volume of compost that can be held by their pots.

Root pruning, a technique used in bonsai, and completely replacing the compost both help to control a tree's size and keep it growing well. Root pruning should be done in late winter or early spring, and it involves trimming back individual roots with secateurs (hand pruners). Shake the old compost from the existing roots before you return the plant to its container so that you can replace all the old compost with fresh compost.

The amount of water applied to the container will cause nutrients to leach from the compost. Although nutrients are easy to add in the form of slow-release, pellet fertilizers, the tree may not be able to absorb them. To improve its uptake, you can add a biostimulant or a mycorrhizal fungi to the compost every two or three years (see pages 72–3).

Planting conifers and palms

Conifers, palms and evergreen trees require more aftercare than deciduous trees planted while dormant, as their foliage will lose water, which they will be unable to replenish until their roots grow out into the soil. For this reason they require additional watering and protection from the sun and wind.

When to plant conifers

Mid-spring, when the soil is moist and warm, is the best time to plant conifers. This allows the plants to establish before winter. However, container-grown conifers can also be planted at other times of year (particularly early autumn), provided they are kept well watered in summer and protected from winds in winter.

If conditions are not immediately suitable for planting when the conifers arrive, plant them in a trench in a sheltered spot (known as heeling in) until conditions improve. Do not take container-grown plants out of their pots until you can plant them properly, or you will risk drying out their delicate roots.

How to plant conifers

Conifers should be planted in the same way as other trees and shrubs, but after planting protect the plants from cold and drying winds by erecting a windbreak.

To do this, insert three stout stakes firmly into the ground, then wrap a windbreak sheet, hessian, or layers of horticultural fleece around the outside of the posts. Tie securely to the stakes and peg down at the bottom to secure. Once the conifer is well established this protection can be removed. Tall trees may also need staking so that they are not blown over by the wind.

Aftercare

Do not feed conifers unless they are showing signs of starvation (unnatural yellowing foliage). If they are given too much food, conifers will grow more quickly, producing lush, often uncharacteristic, growth that does not look attractive and is prone to damage caused by drying and cold winds.

During the winter, some conifers are susceptible to damage caused by the weight of accumulated snow. This can cause the plant either to be pulled out of shape or have limbs broken. You can prevent damage by tying up susceptible plants before winter or routinely knock heavy falls of snow from exposed plants before damage is caused.

HOW TO PLANT A CONIFER

1 Place the conifer in the prepared hole and check the planting depth. The soil mark should be at the same level as the surrounding soil.

2 When the plant is in position, untie the wrapper and slide it out of the hole. Avoid disturbing the ball of soil around the roots.

3 Replace the soil around the plant and firm down to eliminate big pockets of air. Water and occasionally spray the foliage on sunny days.

4 It is worth mulching the ground after planting. It will conserve moisture, and some mulches, such as chipped bark, look attractive.

Pest control

Once established, conifers will largely look after themselves. Mites and aphids can be problems on pines and spruces respectively, causing the needles to drop and producing unsightly bare stems. Aphids are easy to control with insecticidal sprays, but mites are more persistent (you may wish to get in a professional to treat an affected specimen). Mites are particularly active during warm, dry years when conifers are under stress. You can help prevent outbreaks by watering conifers during a drought and spraying the foliage occasionally to increase air humidity. Do this in the evening to avoid scorching the foliage on a sunny day.

When to plant palms

In temperate climates palms are best planted from late spring to late summer so that they are established before winter. However, in more tropical climates palms are best planted during the wet or rainy season and when the soil temperature is above 18°C (65°F).

How to plant palms

Regardless of how the palm tree is bought, initial aftercare is essential for its successful survival and quick establishment. A critical factor for ball and burlapped palms is the ratio between the prepared rootball and the length of the stem. Although some palms can thrive with a shallow rootball, it is often better to buy a palm with a large rootball as this will improve its chances of survival.

When planting the palm tree the principles are the same as planting any other containerized or ball and burlapped tree, although it is important to remember that palms generally prefer well-drained soils.

If water does not drain through the bottom of the planting pit, then plenty of organic material and/or horticultural grit or sand should be dug into the soil. It is critical that palms are not planted any deeper than the depth to which they were originally grown.

Large ball and burlapped palms will require support for the first year until the root system fully establishes. Since traditional techniques can be difficult to master, the triple staking and rubber guy wire system can be used instead (see pages 82–3), although there is also a specialized system that utilizes a metal collar and tensioning wires to provide support. Smaller palm trees require little or no support.

All palms have very large leaves which lose lots of water. To reduce evaporation, the leaves can be tied closely together, or the foliage can be sprayed with water to help cool them during hot weather.

Aftercare

Newly planted palms will require daily watering for the first six weeks after planting, and it is a good idea to spray the leaves with water when watering the rootball to help counteract moisture loss via the leaves while the roots are becoming established.

Although overheating may be less of a problem for container- or pot-grown palms, large ball and burlapped palms, which will have had their crown of leaves reduced by over half to protect the heart of the palm's crown, may suffer. In some species that are difficult to establish, like the sabal palm, the leaves may be removed altogether and will only re-grow as the palm tree establishes.

Generally palms do not require any soil improvement. Although the use of mycorrhizal fungi or soil biostimulants has been shown to increase the rate of establishment, fertilizer should only be added the season after they establish.

Once the root system is established a general NPK 15-5-10 fertilizer can be applied during the growing season. Do not add it too early in the spring, however, as a high-nitrogen feed applied during cool weather will cause the plant to produce soft green growth rather than growing upwards, which may result in stunted growth.

Bad weather damage

The occurrence and extent of winter damage in palms depends on the lowest temperature and the duration of cold. Cold damage appears first in the foliage, and causes the leaves to turn brown and die. However, as long as the root system and crown of the palm survive then the damage may only be superficial. If the root system freezes the palm will not recover. The roots will often tolerate temperatures several degrees cooler than the foliage, so even if the foliage dies there is still a chance that the palm will re-sprout when the temperature rises in spring.

Staking trees

The trunk of a healthy, well-grown tree will exhibit an obvious thickening towards the base. If trees are staked for too long or have been grown too close together, or are simply young, they do not have this reinforcement wood, so they are easily blown over, even during moderate winds. Sometimes, the trunks crack or eventually break. To avoid this, staking is necessary, as it allows the root system to anchor the tree into the surrounding soil.

Types of stake

There are numerous types of stake: they can be round or square in shape, and made from hardwood, softwood, recycled plastics or concrete. As the purpose of the stake is to hold the trunk while the roots colonize the surrounding soil, the stake material is largely irrelevant, although one that will rot and fail over time should be preferred to one that will not. All tree stakes should be removed once the root system has established. The best stakes are made from wood, and most, both hard and softwood, are treated (tanalized) with preservative to prevent them from rotting.

Flexible tree ties allow the trunk of the tree to grow, without harming the tree. The buckle mechanism should always go around the stake, otherwise it will damage the bark. This picture shows a tie being incorrectly fitted.

Types of tree tie

There is a huge range of tree ties available. The most effective ties are those made from a material that has a certain amount of elasticity and can be adjusted. If you are using a single, low, straight stake, an angled stake or the T-bar method, it is important that a rubber cushion or spacer is used to protect the tree from rubbing against the stake.

Most ties have an integral spacer that can be adjusted. Some use a buckle, others lock on themselves and some use Velcro. Whichever tie you use, check it regularly so that it does not rub against or constrict the developing trunk.

When to stake trees

It is often necessary to stake recently planted trees so that they are supported during early growth. However, the staking should be done in such a way that the tree can still move. The stake should be left in place for no more than three growing seasons. If a tree cannot support its own weight after this time it should be pruned hard and a new leader trained. Alternatively, it should be pruned so that it develops into a multi-stemmed tree.

A newly planted tree is staked to allow the root system to anchor and grow into the soil, while allowing the trunk and branches to sway so that reaction timber forms naturally in the trunk. However, if the roots move so that they are no longer in touch with the soil, the tree will fail to establish and diseases may invade the root system.

Some fruit trees require more secure staking when they are trained into a specific shape.

The larger the tree that has been planted, the more substantial the stake should be. A tree that is less than 1m (3ft) tall and that has been planted in a protected site where there is little wind movement will not need a stake. However, a larger tree needs a stake because it will have a small rootball compared to its branch area, which would act like a sail in the wind, and even a small tree may need staking in a very windy site.

Different staking methods

The appropriate way of staking will depend on the type of tree you plant and how it has been grown. Some trees are going to need considerably more support than others, especially if they are planted in exposed sites, such as seaside, mountainous and hilly regions or in wind funnel areas of towns and cities.

In all cases, the stake should be positioned so that the prevailing wind blows the tree away from the stake, not towards it, as this would cause the stake to rub against the trunk and cause damage. Use the following guidelines for choosing a system:

Container-grown trees These trees need either a stake angled at 45 degrees, a T-bar or a three-stake system (see page 82). Specimens over 3m (10ft) tall need an underground or above-ground guying system. Container-grown conifers, evergreens and palms are best with a T-bar.

Bare-rooted trees These trees require a straight, single stake driven in before planting; a stake set at an angle of 45 degrees; or a T-bar or three-stake system. With any of these systems the stake should be no higher than 50cm (20in).

Rootballed trees These need a stake angled at 45 degrees or a T-bar or three-stake system. Specimens over 3m (10ft) tall need an underground or above-ground guying system. The T-bar system should be used for rootballed conifers, evergreens and palms. Use an angled stake whenever you need to protect the rootball.

Multi-stemmed trees These trees require a modified T-bar or three-stake system in order to secure the stems.

Trees planted on a slope Trees planted in this position need an angled stake.

Single stake method shown for a larger bare-rooted tree.

Angled stake method shown for a larger containerized tree.

Single staking

A low single stake is driven vertically into the ground and fixed to the tree with a tree tie. The overall height of the stake should not exceed 50cm (20in) above ground when it is fully driven in. This method is only suitable for bare-rooted trees because the stake can be inserted without causing any damage to the roots.

The stake should be placed with the tree in the planting hole first to find the best position. The tree is then removed so that the stake can be driven in. Once secure, the tree is planted before being tied to the stake.

This is one of the most widely used staking techniques and it can be adapted for use on a variety of different sized trees. Larger trees will require taller stakes, which should be reduced in height or removed once the tree has established.

Angled staking

Suitable for vulnerable container-grown or rootballed trees, angled staking is when a stake is driven into the ground away from the base of a planted tree at an angle of 45 degrees. This technique prevents damage to the root system. About 50cm (20in) of the stake should be above ground. The tree is then securely attached to the stake with a flexible tree tie.

For larger container or rootballed trees a longer angled stake can be used, but should be removed as soon as the tree has established.

Three-stake system shown for a large tree.

Wire guying can be used to support large rootballed or container-grown trees.

T-bar and three-stake system

These methods are becoming increasingly popular, and can be adapted for use in a wide range of situations. They should be used for medium to large trees, whether they are bare-root, container-grown or rootballed plants.

In the T-bar system, two posts are driven vertically into the ground on either side of the planting pit so that about 50cm (20in) of each stake is above ground. A treated wooden horizontal bar is then nailed to the upright bars so that the tree blows away from the cross-bar. The tree is held with a rubberized tie with a spacer to make sure that the trunk does not rub against the cross-bar.

In the three-stake system, three posts are driven into the ground to the same depth as in the T-bar method. However, instead of using a wooden cross piece, three wires or ropes are used, and these are passed through a protective sleeve as they pass around the tree trunk and are fixed to the stakes so the tree can still sway in the wind. Once the tree has established the system should be removed.

Wire guying

This is an expensive method of supporting a tree because it requires specialized equipment. It is mainly used for large rootballed or container-grown standard trees and conifers, but it is not suitable for palms.

After the tree has been planted, three or four bullet-shaped anchors are driven into the ground around the tree. Attached to each anchor is a stainless steel cable. The movement of the cables as they are brought under tension locks the anchors into the ground. Each cable runs through a plastic or rubber sleeve, placed around the trunk of the tree and usually positioned above a branch to stop it from slipping down the trunk. Although the cables support the tree higher up the trunk, they allow it to sway in strong winds.

It is usual to install the cables so that the protective collars do not form a constricting circle around the same area of the trunk. They are usually arranged at various heights from about 1.8m (6ft) up. The cables can be adjusted as the tree grows, and the system usually remains in place for three or four years. When the cables are removed, the ground anchors can be carefully dug out or left in the ground.

Staking with bamboo canes

This method is suitable for small container-grown trees, which require a minimum amount of staking and may need support for only a year. A bamboo can be pushed into the ground at an angle of 45 degrees away from the rootball. The cane is then cut off, leaving about 50cm (20in) above ground. A tree tie attached to the cane and the tree holds it firmly. A spacer may be needed to prevent the cane from rubbing against the trunk and the tie should be checked and loosened from time to time so that it does not become too tight.

Triple stakes and rubber guy wires

An alternative to the wire guying system, this method is less expensive and requires no specialist equipment. It is suitable for palms, conifers and medium-sized standard or feathered trees, whether they are sold as bare-rooted, rootballed or container-grown plants.

Three wooden posts are driven into the ground at equal intervals around the edge of the planting hole after the tree has been planted. The posts should be vertical with 50–75cm (20–30in) remaining above ground. A long, flexible rubber tree tie is attached to one of the wooden stakes, wound around the trunk and attached to the same stake, usually by nailing or stapling. This process is repeated on the other two stakes. The flexibility of the ties allows the tree to sway.

Underground guying

This method is used only on large container-grown or rootballed trees and palms in locations where an above-ground guying system is impracticable – if someone might walk into the cables, for example – or where appearance is important. It requires specialized installation and is invisible when in place. It uses similar ground anchors and cables to the above-ground wire guying method, but instead of being attached to the trunk, the cables are attached to a special collar that fits around the tree's root plate. This allows the trunk to sway freely.

Below-ground staking of palms

Palms have relatively small rootballs and are often transplanted or sold as mature specimens. Their fibrous trunks make it impossible to use a traditional guying system so the below-ground method is used instead. An adjustable, padded steel collar is fitted around the trunk and is then attached to traditional guy wires, installed with the same equipment as for above-ground guying.

Bamboo canes are suitable for staking small, container-grown trees that don't require very strong support.

If you have reduced the number of leaders on a tree, use a stake to encourage the remaining one to grow vertically.

If you are inserting a stake when the tree has already been planted, put it at an angle to avoid damaging the roots.

Watering newly planted trees

Effective and timely watering is the most important factor for the survival of a newly planted tree. Tree roots, especially the microscopic root hairs that absorb moisture from the soil, are easily damaged during planting, no matter how careful you are. For the tree to establish there must be sufficient water both in the tree's rootball and in the surrounding soil so that new roots can grow and proliferate out from the tree.

Misting

In dry and windy conditions newly planted trees will require daily watering, which should be undertaken either in the early morning or in the late afternoon to early evening.

To help cool down the foliage of trees, the leaves can be sprayed throughout the day with a fine mist of water. As the water evaporates from the surface of the leaves it will help cool them down and thus reduce the level of transpiration between the roots and the leaves, conserving water.

Rainwater collected from roofs and stored in water butts does not contain the chemicals that are found in domestic water, and has the added advantage of being free.

Waterlogged ground can easily kill a newly planted tree, so take care not to overwater. If drainage is poor, you may need to improve the soil before planting.

Following planting, apply plenty of water to allow the soil to settle around the roots.

Avoid misting trees in strong sun as the droplets can act like tiny magnifying glasses and burn the foliage. In such conditions drape some shade netting over the tree, and water the soil more regularly.

How much water?

Overwatering, which causes as many new plants to die as underwatering does, is likely to be a problem on ground that is naturally slow to drain, such as clay or compacted soils. In these conditions water little but often, making sure each time that the water has drained away completely. Too much water around the roots will restrict oxygen levels and cause the roots to die.

Water should be applied at the following rate: 2.5cm water per litre of container-grown tree (3.7in per gallon). This means that a 10-litre (2.6-gallon) container-grown tree will require 25cm (10in) of water every day during a dry period.

On poorly drained soils this quantity can be reduced by half, and the total volume of water is best given in two applications, one in the morning and one in late afternoon. If the soil remains wet and soggy between each of the waterings then you are overwatering.

Water drains more easily on light, sandy soils, so you may find you have to apply more water if the tree is planted in this type of soil.

However, you should carefully monitor the water given to rootballed trees planted in sandy soils. This is because they might have been lifted from clay soil, so the water will not drain easily from the rootball into the surrounding sandy soil.

As your tree establishes, water it less frequently so that the tree can be slowly weaned off its reliance on regular artificial watering.

Young trees will require daily watering in windy or dry conditions, but you should take care not to overwater, which restricts the amount of oxygen that can reach the roots of the tree.

Signs of thirst

Evergreen trees and container-grown deciduous trees that are planted out of their dormant season usually require much more aftercare than other trees. This is because they can quickly succumb to drought.

Touching the foliage throughout the day, especially in late morning, will help you determine if the tree is stressed. If the foliage feels warmer than the ambient air temperature then you should lightly water the tree and mist the foliage to cool the leaves.

If the leaves feel noticeably cooler than the air temperature, there is sufficient water available to the roots for it to be drawn up into the trunk, through the branches, and to the leaves. Once it reaches the leaves it evaporates from their surface and keeps them cool.

If there is insufficient water available to the roots the leaves will overheat and, if unnoticed, they can curl and die.

Sunken irrigation systems are available and allow water directly into the root zone.

Watering methods

There are a number of useful devices widely available that will make watering less of a chore during hot or windy weather.

Porous plastic pipes can be installed around the outside of the rootball before planting. These have a reservoir that protrudes above ground so that it can be easily filled to allow water to seep through the pipes into the ground. This type of system minimizes surface evaporation and places the water directly in the soil around the roots.

Another system uses a high-density polythene irrigation bag, which is placed on the surface of the soil and wrapped around the base of the trunk. The bag is then filled with water, which seeps through small holes at the base and into the root zone.

This reduces surface evaporation from the soil, and it can be removed when it is no longer needed, unlike the buried pipes, which cannot be retrieved once installed.

Understanding mulching

After planting a new tree, it is important to minimize the competition for light, water and nutrients from other plants, especially weeds. One of the best ways of keeping the ground clear is to apply a mulch. A mulch is placed on the surface of exposed soil to reduce evaporation, inhibit the germination of annual weeds and, when the mulch consists of a natural material, provide nutrients as it decomposes.

Types of mulch

The most often-used of the natural mulches is composted bark, which is derived from wood waste from the forestry industry, when the material is passed through a chipping machine to break it into small nuggets. The material is graded and composted before being sold. The chips can vary in size and quality because of the different types of tree from which they are derived.

Another popular mulching material is garden compost, made by composting household and garden waste; a similar material is sometimes available also through municipal recycling centres. Other useful materials are coir, shredded newspaper, sawdust, spent hops, farmyard manure and grass clippings, all of which should be thoroughly composted before use. Farmyard manure is particularly good for adding fertility to soil, and garden compost also contains a good range of nutrients.

In nature, the natural woodland floor provides sufficent quantities of mulch in the form of well-rotted leaves and other organic material.

Artificial mulches and mulch mats are made from woven materials, such as polypropylene or other plastics. Woven plastic mats are permeable to air and water, but some types of black plastic matting are not, which means that rain cannot reach the soil. Artificial mulch mats, which may break down or degrade slowly, are unattractive and are often used in conjunction with natural mulches, which are laid on top.

Even if they do biodegrade, artificial mulches, unlike natural mulches, do not supply any nutrients. Their main advantages are that they are long-lasting and are effective at inhibiting the growth of both annual and perennial weeds.

Several natural mulches have been bonded together to form mulch mats that will break down over about two years. Commonly used materials include flax, hemp, sisal and coir fibre. Like other mulch mats, they should be held down with some other material, and they are widely used with organic mulches.

The benefits of mulches

Applying a mulch, whether natural or artificial, has several advantages for newly planted and established trees. Mulches help to keep moisture in the soil by reducing evaporation from its surface, thereby reducing the need for watering.

Overmulching

A mulch that is deeper than 10cm (4in) can create excessive moisture around the root zone and force oxygen out of the soil, and this will stress the tree and increase its susceptibility to root-borne diseases. Piling a mulch against the trunk can cause temperatures to rise as the mulch breaks down, and this may damage the bark, leading to insect infestation or disease. A deep mulch can also be a wonderful habitat for harmful rodents, which eat the bark of new trees.

Mulches that are not properly composted or those containing material that is high in nitrogen, such as grass clippings, can have an effect on the soil's pH or take nitrogen from the soil as they decompose. The continued use of such mulches can lead to nutrient deficiencies.

A mulch 5–10cm (2–4in) thick will also reduce the germination and growth of annual weeds and grasses.

Mulches can be used to protect the roots of less hardy trees by acting as an insulating layer on the surface of the soil and reducing the level of frost penetration into the soil. They can also protect the surface of the soil from high temperatures during summer.

Natural mulches gradually introduce organic matter into the soil, thus improving the water-retaining capacity of light soils, while improving the drainage and aeration on heavier soils. In addition, the beneficial soil fungus and bacteria that invade the mulch to break it down can produce a physical mat of fungi roots (hyphae) that can inhibit the growth of disease-spreading fungi in the area of the root zone. Natural mulches also create the kind of area that would be found around the tree in a forest or woodland, thereby

MULCHING A TREE

1 Grass and other plants growing close to a young or newly planted tree will make it harder for the tree to establish.

2 Tie a loose line around the base of the tree and, using an edging iron, mark out a circle around the tree.

3 Using a garden spade or turfing iron, carefully remove the grass from the circular area around the tree.

4 Carefully remove any perennial weeds and, if the soil is dry, water the area surrounding the tree well.

5 An artificial mulch mat could be used, or simply spread a mulch of bark chips out to the damp line.

6 Make sure that the mulch is not too deep or banked up against the stem, or it may damage the bark.

encouraging natural nutrient recycling. As the mulch decomposes, it encourages mycorrhizal and other nutrient activity, which in turn help the tree's health and vigour.

Mulching around trees helps to reduce the risk of the trunk being damaged by lawnmowers and strimmers. An artificial mulch around an established tree can help to maintain its health by reducing compaction of the root zone, which it does by providing a cushion to protect it from foot or vehicle traffic.

Mulches can give a newly planted tree an attractive and properly planted appearance, keeping down weeds at a time when it is important that nothing competes with the tree for moisture and nutrients.

Applying a mulch

After planting the tree, remove any annual or perennial weeds, including grass. If using a mulch mat, apply this first. Then apply a 5–10cm (2–4in) layer of organic or natural mulch. If the tree prefers acidic soil, mulch with composted pine bark or needles, which will not raise the soil pH or hinder the tree's take-up of nutrients.

If a mulch needs to be reapplied, remove the top layer of the old mulch and place new mulch on top. Check that the final mulch is not too deep and do not pile mulch against the tree trunk as it will prevent air getting to the bark. Instead, rake it back so that it forms a doughnut around the trunk and spreads beyond the edge of the branches or beyond the drip line.

Moving trees

It is of course best to begin by planting a tree or shrub in its final position, but even in the best planned garden mistakes can happen. Moving established plants, even small ones, is hard work and needs careful forethought. However, with a few helpers and good preparation, many plants can be moved successfully.

In gardens where space is limited or where there is close planting, established pruning is required to control the size of a tree and so prevent it from smothering other plants. If, however, the tree does start to outgrow its space, it may need to be moved.

When to move trees

The best time for transplanting most established trees is during the dormant season (late autumn to early–mid-spring), as long as the soil is not waterlogged – in which case digging could damage the soil structure – or frozen, which would make digging impossible. Spring planting gives a full season's growth before the winter; an autumn move allows the plant to develop a good root system before spring. Evergreens, including conifers, are best moved in mid-spring when the soil is moist and warm enough to encourage rapid root growth.

What size rootball?

The rootball diameter and depth will depend on the size of the plant you are trying to move. The diameter should be about the same as the spread of the branches and about one-third the height of a tree. The depth of the rootball depends on the type of soil in your garden. The lighter the soil the more penetrating the roots and so the deeper the rootball will have to be. For example, a 30cm (12in) deep rootball on clay soil may need to be twice that depth on a light, sandy soil. Bear in mind that rootballs with soil attached can literally weigh a ton if you are moving a small tree. Make sure you have sufficient help before you start.

Root pruning

The chances of successfully moving trees can be improved by pruning the roots in advance, a technique known as root pruning. It should be done up to a year before the move.

To root prune, simply dig a vertical trench around the tree, along the line where you plan to dig it up, and sever any roots you find, then refill the trench with soil. The tree will produce more fibrous roots in the soil nearer to the trunk, and these will form part of the rootball, increasing the tree's chances of survival after the move.

Making moves

Before you start, decide on the new position of the tree and prepare the planting hole, which should be about twice as wide and slightly deeper than the rootball. Fork over the bottom of the hole, incorporating a bucketful of grit on heavy soils to improve drainage.

Use a spade to cut a slit-trench around the tree being moved to mark out the size of the rootball and to sever any roots near to the surface. Then cut a second slit-trench about 30cm (12in) further out and dig out the soil in between to form a trench around the specimen. Make this trench as deep as the rootball.

Undercut the rootball from the trench by inserting the spade at an angle of about 45 degrees all the way round. Small rootballs should then be completely undercut and can be wrapped. Larger rootballs may need further excavation to expose any vertical roots under the middle of the rootball.

HOW TO MOVE A SMALL TREE

1 Before moving a tree, make sure that the planting site has been prepared and the hole excavated. Water the plant well the day before moving it.

2 Dig a trench around the tree, leaving a large rootball (the size depends on the size of the tree). Carefully sever any lateral roots that you encounter to release the rootball.

3 Dig under the tree, cutting through any vertical taproots that hold it in place.

4 Rock the tree to one side and insert sacking or strong plastic sheeting as far under the tree as you can get it. Push several folds of material under the rootball. Ask someone to help if you are finding it difficult to do on your own.

5 Rock the tree in the opposite direction and pull the sacking or plastic sheeting through towards you, so that it is completely under the rootball of the tree. Depending on the size of the tree, you may be able to lift the rootball slightly to make this easier.

6 Pull the sacking round the rootball and tie it firmly at the neck of the plant with some string. The tree is now ready to move. If it is a small plant, one person may be able to lift it out of the hole and transfer it to its new site on their own.

7 If, as is likely, the plant plus the soil is quite heavy, it is best moved by two people. Tie a length of wood or metal to the sacking. With one person on each end, lift the tree out of the hole.

8 Lower the transplanted tree into the prepared planting hole. Unwrap and remove the sheeting from the rootball. Make sure that the plant is in the right position, refill the hole, and water well.

After the rootball has been freed, carefully rock it back and slip a sheet of folded heavy-duty polythene or hessian (burlap) under one side, then rock it over the other way and then pull the folded polythene through. Tie the corners of the sheeting over the top of the rootball around the main stem to form a neat package, so that the soil is held firmly. Use rope or strong string to reinforce the rootball on all sides.

Move the tree by pulling on the polythene sheeting, not the trunk. Use a short plank (board) or pair of planks as a ramp out of the hole and then drag it to its new position or get a gang of helpers to lift it. It may be easiest to fix a pole to help carry the tree.

Replant the tree immediately in the prepared hole and water and mulch well. Stake, using one of the techniques described previously, if necessary. Spray the foliage of evergreens after planting and every few days for the first month to help prevent wilting. It is also worth putting up a windbreak around conifers. Keep all transplants well watered throughout their first growing season.

Problems with mature trees

Planting the right tree in the right location and carefully nurturing it can greatly reduce the risk of stress, which is an undesirable state that can lead to the tree being attacked by diseases or pests.

Most trees are completely trouble-free for many years. If you have correctly planted a healthy sapling into well-cultivated soil in an appropriate site, the tree is likely to outlive you without suffering any serious problems. However, if you have acquired a house with a mature tree in the garden you might encounter a few difficulties.

Fighting disease

Trees are highly complex plants that have evolved over millions of years, and they have developed mechanisms to protect themselves against the organisms that cause decay. Their ability to fight off disease depends on the current health of the tree and its inherited resistance.

Trees survive following injury or infection by 'walling off' or compartmentalizing the damaged area to limit the spread of disease to as small a part of their wood as possible. This process of erecting a series of chemical barriers around the area restricts the spread of infection that has entered via a wound to a tree's bark, which might have been caused by careless pruning, a lawnmower or strimmer, the weather or animals.

Some aggressive diseases affect a tree's tissues without a wound, but this is rare and only those trees that are already under stress are likely to be infected.

If the tree is healthy and its boundary-setting processes are good, the decay organism will be halted and the infection will remain localized. If the tree is in poor health and the decay organism is aggressive, the tree's walls may be unable to prevent the decay from spreading, and this may also lead to other, secondary infections, although the decay cannot spread into new stems and branches.

Some trees are able to wall off infection rapidly and effectively. Many trees, in fact, cope perfectly well while having hundreds of infections safely walled off inside their trunks and branches. Those trees that do not respond quickly and effectively often lose an entire branch or may even die. The ability of individual trees to ward off infections is largely hereditary, although the overall health of the tree is also a major factor.

Cavities

A well-established tree can survive for many years with a hollow section in its trunk if the outer layer of sapwood is healthy and continues to transport nutrients from the roots to the branches and leaves. It will be able to survive strong prevailing winds, although if it becomes exposed to wind from the opposite direction – if a shelter-belt is removed, for example – the trunk may twist, causing it to collapse.

Tree defence systems

The natural defence system is known as CODIT (compartmentalization of decay in trees) and has two stages. The first occurs in the tree's living tissue, the vascular bundle, which runs the length of the tree, from the roots to the tips of the branches and the leaves. A tree will resist the spread of an infection by creating barriers above and below the site of the infection and to both sides.

The second stage creates a barrier between the existing wood and the wood that has not yet grown. This is why hollow trees continue to grow and survive.

It was once usual to gouge out the decayed area and fill the cavity with bricks and mortar, but modern practice is to leave the cavity untouched. You should not drill a hole through the cavity to release trapped water because this hole will allow decay from the cavity to spread to the healthy tissue behind it.

The best option is to leave the cavity alone but to check it every year, seeking the advice of a tree expert if necessary, and to improve the vigour of the tree by fertilizing the soil, mulching and, if circumstances dictate, hiring a tree surgeon to inject compressed air in conjunction with mycorrhizal inoculation or biostimulants (see pages 72–3).

Bracing

This is a way of supporting the weight of a branch that might have a natural weakness, such as a codominant stem (see page 106).

Flexible steel support cables were once used to prevent the collapse of branches weakened by decay or narrow forks or to support large, heavy branches. Such cables were often fixed into the living tissue of the tree with eye-bolts. Today, however, non-invasive proprietary systems wrap a sling around the trunk and incorporate elastic shock absorbers that allow the trunks being held to sway.

This type of bracing is expensive and should be considered only for prized trees that cannot be treated in some other way.

This ancient *Quercus robur* (English oak) has managed to survive for centuries, despite having a large cavity in its trunk.

Extreme temperatures as well as some fungal diseases can often cause tree bark to split.

Dead branches at the uppermost canopy indicate there are problems in the root zone.

Pests and diseases

Insect pests and diseases usually affect trees that are already under stress, such as that caused by drought, nutrient deficiency, overpruning or damage to the root system. It is important, therefore, to ensure that your trees are fed regularly and pruned appropriately, if necessary, and that the ground around the base of the trunk is kept clear of weeds and grass.

Successfully tackling a pest or disease depends on identifying the problem in the first instance. If a tree in your garden is clearly not thriving, inspect it carefully for anything unusual.

Symptoms that will suggest that something is amiss include strangely coloured foliage, curled leaves or leaves changing colour early in the year. Liquid oozing from the bark, bark flaking or falling off, swellings or sunken areas on branches or the trunk and any signs of decaying wood should all be investigated immediately.

The organisms causing holes in the bark or leaves can usually be fairly easily identified. Among the culprits are mushrooms and toadstools, which are the fruiting bodies of fungi that have caused or will cause decay and should be identified and dealt with immediately.

Dealing with pests and diseases

The secret to healthy garden trees is understanding their growth habits and providing them with the best possible conditions to allow them to thrive. Carrying out a programme for monitoring and caring for their needs throughout their life is also essential. The aim is to promote a healthy tree, which is more likely to be able to resist disease.

Inspecting trees

Tree inspections are usually carried out by professional tree care specialists, but it would be wise to learn from them and monitor the condition of your trees annually – or more often if you prefer.

Nutrient deficencies

Nitrogen deficiency is common on free-draining soils. A deficiency can manifest itself in a number of ways, but it often appears as off-colour or slightly yellowish leaves or leaves that are smaller than they should be. Apply a high-nitrogen fertilizer (either chemical, such as sulphate of ammonia, or organic, such as dried blood or rotted manure) during late spring and summer.

Phosphorus deficiency is uncommon in gardens, but can occur in acid soils or areas of high rainfall. Growth will be slowed and young foliage dull or yellowish. A fertilizer containing superphosphate, or bonemeal as an organic alternative, will help.

Potassium deficiency is most common in free-draining soils, or those containing a lot of chalk or peat. It causes discoloured leaves, poor growth and reduced flowering and fruiting. Sulphate of potash or wood ash should be applied.

Trace elements are also important for plant health. Applying liquid seaweed extract, either watered in or sprayed on the leaves, ensures a good supply.

A professional tree care specialist may recommend that you mulch around trees in order to conserve moisture in the soil, helping to keep the tree healthy.

Using a hoe to remove weeds from around young trees or shrubs is the surest way of catching them all. It is best carried out in hot weather so that any weeds hoed up die quickly.

Tree inspections should evaluate a number of different things, but special attention should be paid to the condition of new leaves and buds, leaf size and colour, twig growth, the percentage and regularity of dead wood within the crown, as well as spotting any visual warning signs (cavities or poorly attached branches, for example).

If, after an inspection, you think that something is not right, a second opinion may be required. If the inspection is undertaken by a tree care specialist they may recommend a future maintenance programme of preventative care.

This programme may include recommendations concerning the mulching, weed control, irrigation, improving drainage, and fertilizing of the tree. These simple maintenance tasks may be linked to more specialized work such as crown pruning, bracing, tree root aeration and mycorrhizal treatments, or pest and disease control.

Diseases

A plant disease can be defined as an organism (pathogen) or a substance that interferes with and disrupts the normal cycle of growth and in doing so causes visible signs of damage. In addition to diseases there are also disorders such as wind and frost damage or nutrient deficiencies, and these will also limit tree growth and overall health.

Plant diseases can be divided into two very broad groups: those caused by fungi, bacteria and viral pathogens that invade and break down the structure of a tree; and those that are caused by some of the insects and animals that rely on trees for food and shelter.

Tree diseases caused by pathogens generally become more widespread within the tree as it gets older. They can often go unnoticed for many years and eventually cause serious damage. They can also move from tree to tree. It is essential, therefore, to carry out regular inspections.

Mildew

This condition can affect a wide variety of trees and can be separated out into three main categories: downy mildew, powdery mildew and grey mould. Downy mildew is associated with humid weather and shows itself as a fluffy white bloom (fungal hyphae) on the underside of the leaf.

Increasing air movement through the canopy of the tree can reduce the humidity and limit the spread of mildew, as can removing any infected leaves as they appear. Controlling the disease using a fungicide should be a last resort.

Powdery mildew is associated with dry soil and stagnant air. It shows itself as a fluffy, white bloom that usually grows on the upper surface of the leaf, but occasionally on both surfaces. Spraying the foliage with water can reduce the spread, as will fungicidal treatment.

Grey mould is caused by a number of fungal diseases that produce a grey, fuzzy growth on the leaves, which quickly shrivel and die. Control it in a similar way to downy mildew.

Canker

This is caused by a variety of fungi and bacteria, which infect healthy tissue and cause a circular area of the tissue to die and produce a roughly circular wound that harbours the spores, which will re-infect other areas of the tree. Such infected areas may ooze a watery substance, a thick gum or small pustules. Generally, canker infections seldom heal and remain like a weeping sore allowing re-infection to occur.

There are various cankers that are specific to a wide range of trees. They are commonly found on *Aesculus* spp. (horse chestnut); *Castanea sativa* (sweet chestnut); *Cupressus* spp. (cypress); *Ficus* spp. (fig); *Laburnum* spp. (golden rain); *Larix* spp. (larch); *Picea* spp. (spruce); *Pinus* spp. (pine); *Populus* spp. (poplar); *Prunus* spp. (cherry); *Prunus domestica* spp. (plum); *Pseudotsuga menziesii* (Douglas fir); *Quercus* spp. (oak) and *Tilia* spp. (lime).

Many cankers are difficult to control, although removal of the infected tissue or spraying with a fungicide may help to slow the spread of the disease.

Coral spot

The fungus *Nectria cinnabarina*, which causes coral spot, is often found on dead or dying branches, and can also affect weakened or badly pruned branches. The disease cannot penetrate through unbroken bark; it must gain entry via a wound. The disease spreads quickly and produces the typical salmon-pink pustules that erupt through the infected bark.

Limiting infection involves good hygiene, and removing dead wood from the garden. Infected material should be removed back to healthy tissue and the tree regularly sprayed with a fungicide.

Fireblight

This is a serious disease caused by *Erwinia amylovora* and it affects members of the rose family (Rosaceae), including *Sorbus*, *Crataegus*, *Malus* and *Pyrus*.

Infection starts in spring when the disease enters flowers or wounds and quickly spreads through the trunk and branches. Infected branches subsequently die, and always have distinctive dried and shrivelled leaves attached and resemble branches burnt by fire. Part of or the entire tree may be affected, and quick removal of infected branches is recommended.

In areas where fireblight is prevalent it is wise not to grow *Malus* spp. (apple), *Prunus domestica* spp. (plum), *Sorbus* spp. (mountain ash) or *Crataegus* spp. (hawthorn), since these are particularly susceptible. Quick identification and removal of infected material is the only successful method of control.

Coral spot affects broad-leaved shrubs and trees. It causes shoots to die back and produces pink to coral red pustules.

The greyish-white spores of powdery mildew cover the underside of the leaves, making it look like a coating of powder.

Silver leaf

Chondrostereum purpureum is a very common disease of plums and cherries but also affects other members of the rose family including almonds, apricots, apples, pears and hawthorns.

It causes leaves to develop a silvery sheen. Although the leaves are the first sign of the disease they do not spread the disease; instead purplish pustules develop along the bark and increase the infection.

Although many leaves may die, often trees will recover, especially if any dead or dying branches are quickly removed back to healthy tissue. Any regular pruning should be undertaken during summer when the disease is less prevalent.

Anthracnose

This is a common disease in flowering dogwoods, willows, American plane trees, palms, figs, hornbeam, birch, redbud, oak, ash and maples, and it is caused by the fungus *Discula*.

Symptoms vary, but they generally involve leaf spots that develop very small, round silver pustules which spread, causing leaves to die or curl, leading to tip die-back or stem lesions. Quick removal of infected material may slow the spread of the disease through the tree and spraying with a broad spectrum fungicide throughout late spring and early summer helps prevent it occurring.

Honey fungus

A wood-rotting disease caused by *Armillaria*, honey fungus infects stumps and dead wood and can then spread to any stressed or wounded trees in the vicinity via black, threadlike rhizomorphs, commonly called bootlaces. The disease can spread quickly up the trunk and causes a wet ooze to develop.

Susceptible trees include privet, sycamore, magnolia, snowdrop trees, maples, birch and walnut. Removal of infected material is essential to limit the spread. Fungal treatments in the form of root drenches may help, and artificial root barriers may limit the growth of the rhizomorphs, as will mulching around the canopy of garden trees.

The brown area in the centre of this plane leaf indicates anthracnose.

Silver leaf has stained this cherry wood a mid-brown colour.

The fruiting bodies of honey fungus are apparent as they emerge in autumn.

Dutch elm disease

The disease is spread by the elm bark beetle that feeds on stressed trees during the spring, then tunnels into the bark, and infects the tree with Dutch elm fungus, *Ceratocytstis ulmi*. The disease spreads quickly through the tree's branch and trunk section and causes the new shoots and stems to bend over into a crook shape.

Although there is no successful control method there are a number of disease-resistant forms of the elm tree.

Sudden oak death

A disease that was first identified in California, sudden oak death has killed large populations of oaks.

The disease is caused by *Phytophthora ramorum* and *Phytophthora kernoviae* and it has a very wide range of hosts, including *Abies* spp.

Grey mould can cause dead and discoloured patches on leaves and fruit.

(silver fir); *Acer* spp. (maple); *Aesculus* spp. (horse chestnut); *Arbutus* spp. (strawberry tree); *Castanea* (sweet chestnut); *Chaemaecyparis* spp. (false cypress); *Fagus* spp. (beech); *Fraxinus* spp. (ash); *Magnolia* spp.; *Northofagus* spp. (southern beech); *Salix* spp. (willow); *Sequoia* spp. (coast redwood) and *Taxus* spp. (yew).

The disease can induce a range of symptoms but dark lesions on leaves, tip die-back and inverted 'V' shaped rot pattern up the trunk with dark brown-black blotches are common.

Diseased material must be removed completely and destroyed safely, and constant monitoring of nearby plants is essential. There is currently no fungicide effective against this disease.

Grey mould

The fungus that causes grey mould (*Botrytis cinerea*) is the most damaging pest of ornamental container plants as well as conifer seedlings in container tree nurseries. It attacks most species of container seedlings but certain species are particularly susceptible, such as the redwood and giant sequoia, western larch, some pines, Douglas fir, Scots pine, blue spruce, mountain hemlock, noble fir and Alaska-cedar.

This disease can be identified by grey, cottony mycelia and spore masses on the surface of affected shoot tissue. These spore-producing structures show a fuzzy appearance. As the disease progresses, infected shoot tissue becomes watersoaked and brown lesions often develop. The fungus may spread to the main stem, where cankers eventually girdle and kill the shoot.

Phytophthora root rot

This is caused by the fungus *Phytophthora*, which is most problematic in wet or waterlogged soils. The disease produces motile spores that can move through soil water and affect the roots of trees.

The infected roots then die, causing an unexplained death of the crown of the tree. Like sudden oak death a 'V' shaped decay pattern develops with yellow-brown ooze, and the bark dries during summer and can provide an entry point for other diseases.

Removal of infected material and improved drainage to limit the spread of the disease are the best forms of action.

This dead tree may have been killed by sudden oak death, a disease that affects a wide range of trees, and for which there is, as yet, no cure.

Wind damage

This type of damage affects the leaves of a tree, causing them to turn brown and dry up along the edges or curl up and fall off prematurely. The damage is usually noticeably restricted to one side of the tree, and is common in early spring, during summer (especially during periods of drought) and during winter on conifers. Many trees are especially prone during early spring as the emerging leaves are easily damaged. This problem is common in Japanese maples, coffin and bean trees.

Frost damage

This is similar to wind damage, although it is often widespread across the entire canopy of the tree and causes die-back of some younger shoots. It causes the entire leaf to shrivel, often turning black and dying, with the leaves remaining attached.

Any tree can be damaged, but walnuts, bean trees, redbuds, magnolia, golden rain tree and southern beech are susceptible. Avoid planting these in frost pockets and wrap small trees in horticultural fleece in winter.

The flowers of spring-flowering magnolias may be turned brown by frost.

Ladybirds (ladybugs) help to keep garden pests in check.

Crown gall and witches' broom

A common occurrence in many trees, crown gall looks unsightly, but will seldom cause any long-term harm.

The disease is caused by the bacterium *Agrobacterium tumefaciens*, which causes the bark to rupture and new growth to swell and burst from the stem. It tends to be more problematic on poor-draining soils where the bacteria can gain easier access to the tree. Infected areas should be pruned back rigorously to healthy wood and any clippings must be destroyed.

Witches' broom, a similar disease to crown gall, is caused by the fungus *Tuphrina*, or by microscopic mites. The effect is similar and causes irregular growth of hundreds of new shoots that originate from one point along the stem, making it look like the end of a broom.

Trees sometimes show unusual growth patterns in response to environmental conditions. Here, the growth of a tree has been affected by the wind.

Animals that cause harm

Many insects, mammals and birds can cause injury and damage to trees by eating or burrowing into the leaves, feeding on the tree sap and creating an entry point for other pathogens such as fungal spores to enter. They also burrow into the bark and affect the structure of the tree.

Most insect problems are not life-threatening to the tree unless the insect can rapidly multiply its numbers and cause serious problems by repeatedly defoliating the tree.

Control of insect pests is based on the understanding of their life cycle and how to disrupt their breeding patterns so that their numbers never escalate out of control. This can be achieved by integrated pest management which utilizes physical control such as removing infected material quickly, or washing off or hand removing the pest, as well as encouraging or introducing natural

Spider mites produce a very fine webbing on the surface of leaves.

predators to limit their numbers, and if all this fails then the last resort, the use of pesticides.

Aphids

These small green, brown or black insects suck sap from buds and the underside of leaves, especially new growth, and cause them to shrivel. They also excrete sticky honeydew, which can encourage sooty mould.

Removing the infected leaves can help control the spread, along with using biological controls such as the parasitic wasps *Aphiduis* and *Aphidoletes* that lay their eggs into adult aphids. Encouraging other predators such as hoverflies and ladybirds can also help. Spraying with insecticidal soap or using an insecticide should be done before the winged adults appear and colonize other trees.

Scale insects

These tiny insects have semi-hard or hard shells that resemble oyster shells. The females can initially fly, then form their shell and stay in one place to feed. They are often found clustered along young branches and on new leaves. Removal is difficult due to their shell, but spraying with insecticidal soap, horticultural oil, or a systemic pesticide will help.

Red spider mites

These tiny, red or brownish, spider-like pests feed on the underside or surface of the leaf and spin a very fine web that covers its surface. Tiny yellow dots appear on the leaf, and when the number of mites increases the leaf can turn brown and shrivel up. *Phytoseiulus*, a predatory mite, is used as a biological control, or you can spray with insecticidal soap or an insecticide.

Caterpillars

These small creatures come in many shapes and sizes and they can affect our garden trees primarily by chewing the leaves or shoots.

Of the many species that cause significant damage, one of the most serious is the Gypsy Moth which has devastated deciduous oak forest along the eastern seaboard of the USA. The female adult moth is a silvery white with occasional brown and black, bark-like markings; the males are brown in colour.

The voracious caterpillars are hairy and black-bodied with blue spots near the head and red spots on the lower body. They feed on oak, hemlock, maple, apple, alder, black gum, fir, pine, walnut and bean tree.

Trees can be defoliated during summer and, if defoliated twice, can die. Most conifers die after being defoliated once. A biological control is *Bacillus thuringiensis*, a bacterium that grows inside and kills the caterpillars. Predatory beetles are also used. During large outbreaks aerial spraying with an insecticide can be effective. In a garden setting insecticide can be used.

A wide variety of other caterpillars also feed on leaves and cause damage by chewing the edges of the leaves or by removing the middle or just part of the leaf. Other caterpillars stay in colonies, or build a spider-like web to protect themselves, while others curl over the leaves and seal the opening with silk to protect themselves from predators.

Effective control can involve the use female pheromone traps to trap male butterflies and moths. Useful biological controls include *Bacillus thuringiensis* and nematodes, and you can also spray the caterpillars with insecticide when they first appear. Hand removing the eggs before they hatch will also control infestations.

Leaf miners

Commonplace on birch, elm, alder, hawthorn, oak, locust, strawberry trees and maples, these pests will also affect a variety of other trees. Leaf miners are the juvenile offspring of either sawflies, or beetles that lay their eggs in between the layers of a leaf. The larva then tunnels inside the leaf, devouring the soft tissue. The leaves become discoloured and distorted and may fall early, but usually after the larvae have hatched.

Caterpillars can cause visible damage to leaves of trees as they feed.

Hand removal of affected leaves can control the disease, as can spraying with a systemic pesticide. Sticky traps can also be used against the adults.

Leaf-eating beetles

Like caterpillars, a wide variety of adult beetles and their larvae feed on trees. Flea beetles are very small, metallic black beetles that can hop. They eat out uneven shaped notches from the leaves and can even defoliate trees.

Fuller rose beetles devour the young shoots and leaves of maples, persimmon, palms, peach, oaks and pears. In doing so the rusty brown beetles are evident along with their numerous droppings.

Japanese beetles are widespread and will feed on the foliage and shoots of Japanese maples, birch, elm, willow, American sycamore, dogwoods and hollies. The adults are quite large with metallic green heads and coppery-red wing cases. The damage appears as numerous small holes in the leaf that are surrounded by a brown edge.

The vine weevil and other weevils cause distinctive notched damage along the leaf edges as they feed during the evening. Pheromone traps are fairly effective, as are sticky traps to catch the mobile males, and systemic insecticides will provide some control.

Leaf-cutting ants

Like leaf-eating beetles, leaf-cutting ants can defoliate trees, in some extreme cases completely stripping them of leaves in just a few hours. Affected trees are usually within sight of the nest, and you may be able to see the ants themselves carrying the leaves. There may also be a trail of leaf fragments along the foraging path.

Leaf-cutting ants are difficult to control, since they feed on fungus that grows on the leaves, rather than the leaves themselves, so they do not respond to insecticides that are applied to the leaves.

Acephate dusts and insecticide granules are among the more effective controls available, and should be applied directly to the nest openings, according to the manufacturer's instructions. These treatments may not be totally effective, however, and several applications may be required.

Leaf-cutting ants can potentially strip a tree of leaves in just a few hours.

Bark boring beetles

The ambrosia beetle or shothole borer is found boring into the trunk of young maples, hazels, dogwoods, sassafras and hornbeam. The adult beetles are flat, 3mm (1/8in) long with a distinct flat head, and they bore into the trunk of trees and produce an effect as if the trunk has been shot with a shotgun.

Leaf diseases

The diseases that can affect leaves are very varied and can include leaf blotches, tar spots, leaf blisters, peach leaf curl and a number already covered, like anthracnose. Most leaf diseases are caused by fungi, viruses or mites and they are seldom severe enough to cause the tree any lasting damage although their effects can look unsightly. If infected leaves fall prematurely they are best disposed of safely and not composted.

Improving the vigour of a tree by keeping a close eye on its growing environment will help to limit the disease as spraying is expensive and will not resolve the current infection.

Keep a look out for the early signs that a pest, disease or disorder may be present. Small-scale scarring or discoloured leaves could be an indicator.

Birch borers cause serious damage to the bark of birch trees in the USA, as this bronzy coloured beetle lays its eggs under the bark, which hatch into larvae that consume the bark as they grow. The beetle seeks out stressed trees, especially those suffering from the heat of summer. Pheromone traps can be used against adults, and planting non-susceptible species is advised.

Grubs and larvae

Chafer grubs are semicircular, whitish, and have copper-coloured legs and head. The eggs hatch in the soil and develop into grubs which then feed on the roots of trees. Although this is never fatal, it can restrict the growth of young trees. A bacterial biological control will effectively deal with chafer grubs.

The grubs of the adult weevil can also cause a problem to tree roots, especially on young trees. The grubs are whitish in colour, with a copper head with black mandibles, but without visible legs, unlike the chafer grubs. The larvae can be controlled by bacteria or nematodes.

Deer can cause serious problems for trees. Not only do they consume large amounts of foliage, but they can also damage the bark.

Bark boring birds

Sapsuckers and woodpeckers cause some superficial damage to trees as they bore into the trunk in search of insect grubs. They will bore into a variety of trees including maple, birch, conifers, magnolia, apples, willow, palms, grevilleas and locust.

Occasionally trees may be killed if birds ring-bark the trunk and they can also open up wounds to other decay organisms. Control involves the use of a bird scarer, protecting the bark of susceptible trees, or planting trees not commonly affected.

Squirrels cause extensive damage by stripping bark from the trunk and branches of trees.

Rabbits can be problematic as they will feed on young trees and ring-bark older trees.

Mammals

Deer, rabbits and squirrels can cause quite serious damage especially to young trees, by eating the bark, shoots or foliage. Evidence of their work can be seen by the level of damage to the trees, their footprints or droppings.

Fencing or protecting young trees is the best line of defence, along with live traps, scarers or scented deterrents to keep them away from garden trees.

Pruning trees

Some gardeners dislike the idea of pruning, or feel there is so much mystique attached to it that they prefer not to undertake it at all. This, however, may not be in the tree's best interests.

Fortunately, established trees rarely need pruning unless they have dead, diseased or damaged branches or have outgrown their allotted space. It is not the same for young trees, which may greatly benefit from formative pruning. Pruning when they are young allows them to develop a strong leader and a good framework of branches in the canopy, all of which leads to a healthy, robust tree with a beautiful, well-proportioned shape.

Although pruning on mature trees is usually carried out for cosmetic reasons, when it comes to productive trees, such as those that bear fruit, there are also other good reasons for it, since these trees need annual pruning if they are to continue to crop reliably.

The careful choosing, siting and pruning of trees produces the most stunning effects in the garden – whether grandly formal, as shown here, or otherwise.

Tools and equipment

These can be divided into four groups. There are those that perform the cuts, such as saws, secateurs (pruners) and knives; those that are used for clearing up, such as rakes, forks and shredders; safety equipment; and finally the means to gain access to taller plants, such as ladders and towers. They can further be divided into manual tools and powered ones, such as hedge trimmers and chainsaws.

Wear safety gloves to protect your hands when pruning. Use a proper pruning saw to cut thicker branches. Avoid using carpenters' tools as they are not suitable for pruning.

Be extra careful when working at heights. Use a wide-based stepladder for extra stability. If this is not possible, ensure that someone holds the ladder at the base to keep it steady.

Cutting equipment

The most essential tool is a good pair of secateurs. These should be kept sharp. Poor-quality ones, with blades that move apart when you cut, or blunt ones will tear the wood as it passes through. They may also crush and bruise the wood. To a skilled user, a sharp knife can replace secateurs in certain instances.

Long-arm pruners are secateurs on an extension arm that can reach into tall shrubs or trees but are operated from ground-level. For wood thicker than 1cm (½in) a pair of long-handled pruners can be used, and for anything more than 2.5cm (1in) thick you should use a saw.

Saws come in a variety of shapes and sizes. Small folding saws are the most useful for the small-garden owner. These are usually very sharp and remain so for some years. Instead of sharpening, as one used to do, it is usual to buy a new one when it begins to blunt.

Bow saws and even chainsaws may be necessary in larger gardens. Some of the folding saws can be attached to extension arms so that higher branches can be removed without the need for ladders.

Shears are useful for hand-clipping hedges or shearing over certain shrubs such as lavender or ground cover. They are generally used for topiary where curves and trickier corners are concerned. You can also use sheep-shearing shears, but these are not the easiest things to use and scissors are easier for really intricate pieces.

Power tools

In small gardens it may be unnecessary to use power tools, but in a larger one they can be a boon. The crucial thing about such tools is to use them sensibly. Make certain that you know how to operate them and that you are well protected. If you are uncertain about your abilities, have any work that entails their use done by professionals.

Chainsaws are probably the most dangerous tool and should be used only if you have taken a course on their use. It is also very important that power tools are kept in good condition. They should be serviced professionally at least once a year. The settings and running of the engine should be checked and the cutters sharpened. Do this in advance of when you will next need them.

You can get power secateurs but these are very expensive and really useful only if you have a very large orchard and have a lot of fruit pruning or a vast amount of roses to keep in shape.

Clearing up

Most tools needed for this, such as rakes, brooms, forks, wheelbarrows and carrying sheets, should be available as part of the general garden toolkit. Another piece of power equipment of general use to the pruner is the shredder, which will reduce all the waste to small pieces suitable for composting or mulching. Electrically powered equipment is cheaper but generally less powerful and less manoeuvrable; petrol-driven machines tend to be heavier but are more mobile and therefore more suitable for larger gardens.

You also need to exercise discretion if you opt to burn prunings. Bonfires should be lit at dusk and must be supervised at all times. Check with your local council to see if there are any legal restrictions on bonfires in your area.

PRUNING EQUIPMENT

Most gardeners can prune the majority of their plants with just a pruning saw and a pair of secateurs (pruners), but the larger the garden and the more varied the jobs, the larger the collection of tools you will need. It is well worth investing, for example, in a long-arm chainsaw or hedge trimmer if you have tall hedges or trees that need tackling.

Safety

Observing safety precautions is very important if accidents are to be avoided. The operator should always be fully protected, with ear protectors, goggles, hard hats, gloves and boots with steel toecaps all being very important. A hard hat that also includes a face shield and ear protectors is a very good idea.

Providing bystanders with safety equipment should not prove necessary, as they should be kept well out of harm's way at all times. When you are wearing ear protectors, someone may approach you undetected, so always keep a sharp eye out. If your hat takes a heavy knock from a branch, replace it, as the impact may have impaired its strength.

SAFETY EQUIPMENT

To be an effective gardener, you need to garden safely. Always wear protective clothing to avoid serious injuries to your head, limbs, eyes, ears, hands and feet.

An introduction to pruning

Many people feel that, far from nurturing the tree, they are harming it by severing limbs and removing fruit before it has had time to ripen. In fact, the opposite is the case. Pruning can create well-proportioned, healthy trees and removing unripe fruit improves the size and quality of the remainder.

General principles

Nursery-grown trees are occasionally furnished with lower branches almost to the ground. Although these make the tree appear well-proportioned and attractive, and such trees can make good lawn specimens when young, they are seldom appropriate as garden trees because we usually want to grow something else below them. Nursery-grown standards should have clear trunks. Those used as a garden or shade tree will need to have about 2.4m (8ft) clearance on their trunks.

Street trees must be pruned so that they have at least 5m (16ft) clearance for pedestrians or traffic. On the other hand, a tree planted as a lawn specimen, focal point, grown to obscure an eyesore or act as a windbreak may have branches sweeping almost to the ground, and would be termed feathered.

An attractive group of silver birches, *Betula pendula*, that might have benefited from a little more attention with initial training so that they grew more upright.

The lateral branches contribute to the development of a sturdy, well-tapered trunk so it is important to leave some of these lateral branches in place, even though they may be pruned later. Removing the branches too early would restrict the trunk's development.

The spacing of branches, both around and up the trunk, should be encouraged from the start. Branches selected as permanent framework or scaffold branches must be evenly spaced along the trunk and should grow out spirally to produce a well-balanced crown.

It is important to prevent two main branches from originating from the same side of the trunk or almost directly on top of each other. These can be easily removed from a young tree, but if they have been allowed to develop they are best left alone, because removing large branches creates wounds that heal slowly and may make the tree more susceptible to disease.

In general, never remove more than one-quarter of the total leaf area of a tree during pruning. Overpruning can lead to the production of thin shoots from the wounds, known as epicormic or adventitious shoots. These have to be cut away before they develop or they will leave unsightly scars when they are eventually removed.

When to prune

The timing of pruning is a matter of much debate. In the past it was considered a winter job, often because there were fewer demands on the gardener's time than in spring and summer.

However, summer pruning has become more popular as it is now recognized that a tree can heal itself more quickly when it is actively

Unusual trees, such as this weeping cherry, need special attention or they will lose the quality that makes them such an attractive feature in the garden. Regular, careful thinning should achieve this.

growing and has more energy to protect itself. Another advantage of summer pruning is that you can see how much canopy cover has been removed.

Some trees, such as *Betula* (birch), *Acer* (maple) and *Juglans* (walnut), produce heavy sap flows in late winter and early spring as they begin to re-grow after the winter dormancy, so these are best pruned when the tree is in full leaf.

Trees belonging to Rosaceae (the rose family), such as apples, pears, plums and cherries (including ornamental forms), can be affected by a disease called silver leaf (see page 94), which infects wounds in late summer, so these trees are best pruned in early summer.

How to prune

The position of pruning cuts is crucial. On established trees where there is dead wood, a branch should be removed just beyond the branch collar, which is a swelling of the bark around the base of the branch where it joins the tree. The branch collar is part of the trunk and not part of the branch, and it must remain intact. To achieve this, draw an imaginary line parallel to the trunk from the end of the branch bark ridge through the branch. This is where the branch would naturally heal if it were removed. If the tree were growing in the wild and the branch died back, it would be at this point that the tree would sever its connection with the branch.

When we prune a tree, we should aim to follow these natural lines. Do not cut into or otherwise damage this area. Cutting too close to the trunk will breach the tree's natural defences and allow disease to spread.

When you are pruning larger branches, remove some of the weight of the branch before you make the final cut (see page 106). If you are training a branch or trying to change its direction it has to be cut back to a lateral branch or bud.

This may cause masses of new shoots to develop, which will, in turn, have to be reduced in number, but the process is essential if you want to redirect a young branch to train it in a different direction. Pruning early in the tree's life will result in small wounds that will heal fairly quickly.

The beauty of this *Pinus densiflora* (Japanese red pine) is shown to its best advantage as a neatly pruned and well-positioned lawn specimen.

Natural target pruning

This type of pruning involves locating the position of the branch collar. However, before removing the whole branch, it is important to remove part of it first, so that its weight does not cause the bark and branch tissue to tear past the pruning cut if the branch falls to the ground.

A fairly small branch can be simply cut to remove about three-quarters of its length in one or two goes. Branches thicker than about 2.5cm (1in) across should be tackled more carefully.

Begin by making a small cut on the underside of the branch. About 5cm (2in) away from the undercut (which is closer to the trunk) on the upper side of the branch, cut through from the top to remove the branch. Next, locate the branch bark ridge and imagine a point just in front of it. The next target is the lower point where the branch collar joins the branch, which will feel like a bulge just before the branch starts.

Imagine a line between the two: this is where the final cut is made. If either target is not obvious, cut 2.5cm (1in) beyond the branch bark ridge.

Codominant stems

Upright, columnar or fastigiate trees naturally have branches that grow at tight angles to the trunk. If two branches grow from the same point and are left to develop (become codominant), as the tree grows, bark becomes trapped in the angle between them.

So that a single dominant leader develops in the centre of the tree, other branches that might compete with the leader should be removed. Some species that develop a round-headed shape usually have a strong leader and should be allowed to develop naturally. However, some species develop double leaders, known as codominant stems, which can lead to structural weaknesses, so one of these stems should be removed while the tree is young.

Codominant stems occur when two or more main stems (leaders) of about the same diameter grow from the same location on the main trunk of the tree. As the tree grows older, the stems remain similar in size without any single one becoming dominant, which can lead to structural weakness.

REMOVING A LARGE TREE BRANCH

1 Make a cut about 20–25cm (8–10in) out from where the final cut will be on the underside of the branch. Cut about a third of the way into the branch.

2 Make a cut about 10cm (4in) nearer the position of the final cut, cutting until the branch snaps. The initial undercut prevents the wood splitting or bark from stripping.

3 Position the saw for the last cut to avoid damaging the swollen area at the base of the branch. The cut will heal in a couple of seasons. No wound painting is necessary.

Codominant stems or branches originate from the same point on a tree and are usually about the same thickness. Although some codominant stems are naturally quite strong, others are not. When the bark of the trunk or the branch turns upwards, the trunk will have a strong union.

However, if the bark of the trunk turns inwards, the union will be weak. The closeness of the angle is not necessarily an indication of weakness, although in general the tighter the angle between the two branches, the weaker the union is likely to be.

If the union fails, the bark and underlying tissue will often tear along the entire length of the trunk unnoticed, because the downward-pointing bark hides the start of a large structural crack.

Before you remove a codominant stem, cut back the branch to remove the weight. Then make a 45 degree cut from the top of the branch bark ridge to the base of the codominant branch. Some trees might suffer additional die-back because the tree cannot compartmentalize in the same way as it can with a normal branch, but wound tissue will develop under the cut and seal the wound.

HOW TO TRAIN A STANDARD BIRCH TREE

1 Most birch trees develop a natural shape without any intervention, so there is not much pruning required.

2 However, if there are any unwanted branches, as at the bottom of this particular tree, then they should be cleanly removed.

This branch has been pruned too close to the branch collar. This may result in a disease being able to penetrate the tree's natural defences and cause serious problems.

Early removal of branches along the main trunk while a tree is young will result in a clear stem that will show little evidence of puning as the tree ages.

Newly planted trees

The only pruning that should be carried out on a newly planted tree should be limited to correcting any urgent problems while the tree is still relatively young.

Dead, diseased or damaged branches should be removed, although if you have bought the tree from a reputable supplier this should not be necessary. Otherwise, formative pruning should be left until the subsequent years.

The temptation to reduce the crown to compensate for root loss should be avoided, because trees need their canopy and leaves to photosynthesize and the woody stems and branches are used to store energy, which the tree uses to grow.

Establishing a sound structure

A good structure of main framework branches is essential and should be encouraged by formative pruning while the tree is young. The goal of formative pruning is to establish a strong, clear trunk with sturdy, well-spaced branches and a balanced crown. The structural strength of the branches depends on their relative size, the angles at which the branches grow and the spacing between the limbs.

Some species, such as *Quercus robur* (common oak), are comparatively easy to train so that they have a good crown and branch structure. Other trees, however, including fastigiate forms, such as *Populus nigra* 'Italica' (Lombardy poplar), have a dense, upswept crown with many tightly angled branches. Attempting to create a well-balanced, open crown on such a tree would be pointless. With such columnar trees, formative pruning should focus on removing dead, crossing and structurally weak branches while maintaining the tree's natural shape and habit.

Good formative pruning has resulted in a well-cleared trunk, which shows off the distinctive silvery bark for which this beautiful birch is valued.

PRUNING A MULTI-STEMMED TREE

YEAR ONE Cut through the trunk of a suitable feathered tree at the height at which you want the multiple stems to start.

YEAR TWO After a year, select the most suitable stems in order to create a balanced tree and remove the rest.

YEAR THREE Continue to train the individual main stems by removing any dead wood or branches that cross or rub against each other.

Pterocarya stenoptera grows as a suckering tree in the wild, a habit it retains in our gardens, but will still require some pruning.

Pruning multi-stemmed trees

Some trees naturally form multiple trunks and tend to look rather like overgrown shrubs. In fact, they are often regarded by gardeners as shrubs, rather than trees. The number of trunks can vary from just two or three stems to what amounts to a thicket.

The initial formative pruning required to create a multi-stemmed tree is relatively simple. If you have a young, single-stemmed tree, you just have to be bold and cut through the main stem just above ground level, or at whatever height you want the division of the multiple trunks to begin.

Once new growth appears from the base, select the required number (three or more) of shoots and remove all of the others. These remaining shoots will form the basis of your tree, so select the strongest growing ones to make a balanced tree. Continue to train these as you would a tree with a single stem, removing diseased, dead and weak or crossing growth.

Not all trees will shoot from the base after such drastic action, but a surprising number will. You should be selective, as not all trees look very good with multiple stems, although those with highly ornamental bark usually do look attractive.

The best species for training by this method are: *Acer griseum* (paperbark maple); *Acer* x *conspicuum*; *Acer* 'White Tigress'; *Albizia* spp. (silk tree); *Betula* spp. (birch); *Embothrium coccineum* (Chilean fire bush); *Halesia* spp. (snowdrop tree); *Jacaranda mimosifolia*; *Lagerstroemia* spp.; *Platanus* spp. (plane); *Salix* spp. (willow); and *Stewartia* spp.

Multi-stemmed trees, such as this *Acer palmatum* (Japanese maple), grow less tall than single-trunked trees, and their bushy shape can make them an attractive feature.

Maintenance pruning

After the initial training, most trees need only a check-up once or twice a year. In many cases no work will actually be necessary, but if problems do arise, you need to know how to deal with them in good time.

The three Ds

A healthy tree is a far safer one – as well as a prettier one – so it is vital that you perform an annual survey of all the trees you have in your garden. This involves the three Ds – checking for diseased, damaged and dead wood. Any that is found should be cut out cleanly. It is a good idea to check at the end of the growing season, in autumn, and again after the winter as strong winds and frost may have damaged the trees.

Fallen branches should have the snags cut off and any tears should be cleaned up with a sharp knife to remove loose wood. Any heavy branches that are to be removed should be cut off in sections to prevent splitting and tearing caused by the whole weight of a branch being removed in one go. There is no need to dress wounds, even those left by the removal of large branches.

Most trees at some point produce branches that cross others, creating congestion and often wounds where the bark of one rubs against that of another in the wind. Any such

Using secateurs is a quick method of removing suckers, but you must ensure that they are cut out where they are attached to the tree or they will simply grow back.

In gardens where space is limited or where there is close planting, regular pruning is required to control the size of a tree so that it can fill its allotted space and allow other plants to flourish around and below it.

Any dead or dying branches should be clearly cut back to their point of origin, or a point where no damage is visible.

DEALING WITH EPICORMIC SHOOTS

1 Some trees – lime (*Tilia*) in particular – produce what are known as water shoots or epicormic shoots on their trunks.

2 The best way of dealing with them is to rub them out with your fingers as soon as you see them.

crossing wood should be removed. If you are creating a branch-headed standard, then it is also a good idea to thin the timber in the centre of the tree so that air and light can circulate.

From time to time, it is likely that a tree will throw out some wayward growth: an odd stem will suddenly shoot off into space, spoiling the shape of the tree. These should be removed at some point within the shape of the tree. Similarly, if the tree is a variety with variegation or non-standard foliage, it may throw out reverted stems, with leaves that are plain green, and these stems should be removed.

Epicormic shoots and suckers

Some trees produce water (epicormic) shoots. These are shoots that appear around wounds where, for example, a branch has been removed or where a lawnmower has damaged the bark at the base of the trunk. Rub these epicormic shoots out at their base.

If the tree has been grafted, any shoots that appear from below the graft union should be removed, even if they look as though they are in the ideal place, as these will be different from the rest of the tree.

Similarly, suckers often appear from below ground. These may come from a grafted rootstock or just as a natural suckering habit. Unless you want to develop a multi-stemmed tree, these should be removed right back to their point of origin. It may even be necessary to carefully dig back below soil level in order to get rid of them.

Controlling size

There is nothing more magnificent than a tree that has been allowed to grow to its full size. You have only to visit an arboretum to see how majestic they look. However, this is often not always possible in the average garden due to various considerations, but predominantly those of space and shadow.

In many cases, controlling the size of a tree is simply a question of removing a few side branches, but in other cases, it may mean reducing the height of the whole tree. One way of doing this is a technique known as 'drop-crotching', a form of thinning used to reduce the size of large trees, which involves the removal of a main branch (or leader) by cutting it back to a large lateral branch. The original outline of the tree is kept the same but it is much reduced in size.

This should only be done once the tree has reached its full size but when the branches are still young, so that the shaping will not be too unsightly. On a large tree it might be best to leave this job to a professional arborist, who may undertake the reduction over two or more years.

Crown raising or lifting

Raising the crown of a tree is undertaken to allow clearance below the lower branches to allow other plants to grow beneath them, to enhance or expose a view, to allow more of the trunk to be seen, to allow vehicle or pedestrian access or to clear branches away from utilities.

The distance from top to bottom of the canopy should be at least twice the length of clear trunk that remains after pruning. For example, a 10m (33ft) tall tree should have branches on the top 7m (23ft), which would mean that the maximum height to which the crown should be raised would be 3m (10ft).

Crown raising or lifting can involve the total removal of a branch to lift the canopy. Sometimes it is done more subtly by removing some of the lateral growth, lightening the weight, which will naturally lift the branch. A mixture of branch lifting and removal is usually required. The process can be undertaken in summer or winter.

Crown thinning

Mainly used on broadly spreading established trees, crown thinning allows greater light to penetrate through the canopy, which is particularly useful if you want the light to be directed towards any shrubs or perennial plants growing beneath the tree.

The aim is to lighten the interior of the branch structure by removing smaller branches, but to avoid overpruning by never removing more than one-quarter of the total crown area. Overpruning will cause stress and lead to the excessive growth of epicormic shoots, which is the way a tree forces dormant buds to grow in order to increase its leaf area.

To avoid stressing the tree, crown thinning should be carried out over several years. During the process, any codominant stems with weak connections should be removed, allowing dominance to return to the remaining stem. Structural problems, such as weak-growing, diseased or rubbing branches, can be rectified at the same time, and all pruning should be to a branch collar or ridge.

Crown thinning is best undertaken when the tree is in full leaf in mid- to late summer, when the tree will heal quickly. It is seldom carried out on conifers, unless a tree has lost its main leader, when it is important to remove dominance from the other branches by training a new leader.

Crown reduction

When a tree is losing vigour because of old age and the canopy is beginning to die back, the dead ends of branches

CROWN RAISING More light can be obtained below a tree by removing some of the lower branches so that the light from above is able to shine through and down the canopy.

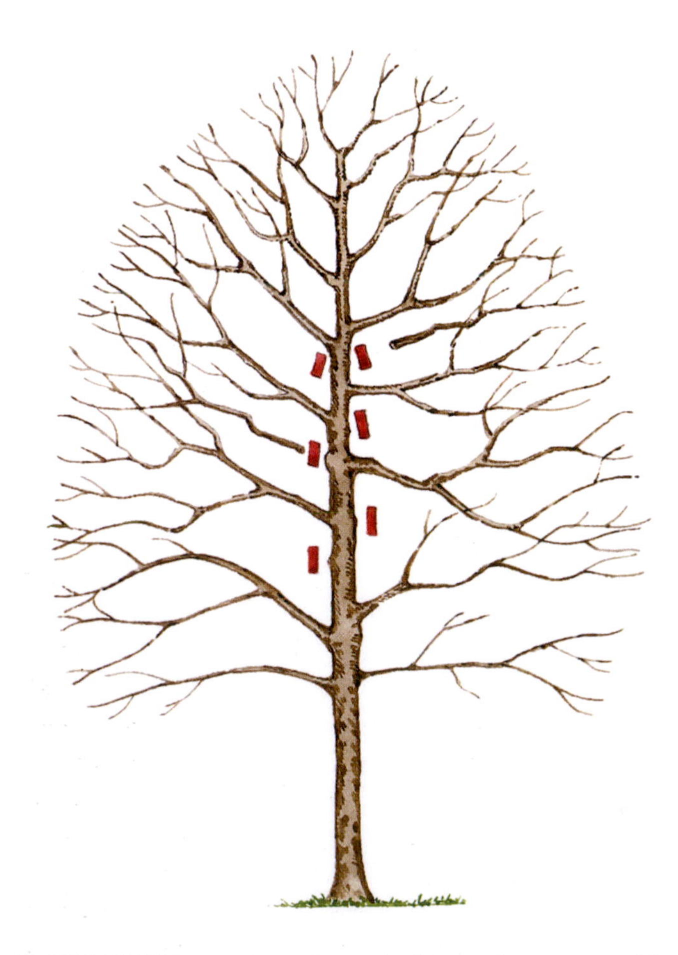

CROWN THINNING An alternative method is to thin out some of the branches from the crown area so that dappled light is able to filter its way down through the canopy of the tree.

can be seen projecting above the leafy canopy, which is sometimes known as stag heading. In such cases, or if a tree has simply grown too large, crown reduction may be necessary.

Crown reduction is also called 'drop-crotching' because the branches are pruned back to a fork in the branch – a crotch – further back down the stem so that its overall length is reduced. The end result should look natural, and the canopy a pleasing shape but smaller in height and spread.

Crown reduction is a long process and requires considerable skill. As with other methods of pruning established trees, the total area of removed foliage and branches should not exceed one-quarter of the total area of the canopy. Crown reduction is best carried out in summer, although on old trees it is often done in winter as it is easier to see the outline of the branches.

Topping

This is a method of reducing the overall height of a tree by about one-quarter. It is mostly used to clear branches away from power lines, but it can be carried out in the garden to keep a tree smaller.

It is an aggressive type of pruning that severely stresses the tree and causes epicormic growth, so it should only be done when absolutely necessary. The multitude of pruning cuts and the fact that a lot of foliage is removed often make the tree susceptible to disease.

Topping is considerably more damaging than pollarding because it is conducted less frequently, and problems occur as the epicormic branches develop, since they are not connected as securely as naturally formed branches.

The delightful weeping habit of a weeping willow has been delicately pruned here to provide a view and frame the seat that has been positioned around the trunk.

Ageing trees

Trees are capable of outliving humans by centuries. Indeed, some English yews are estimated to be as much as 4,000 years old, their presence spanning many ages of time and history. The potential lifespan of a tree varies greatly. With oaks, it can be several hundred years, while in the case of birches, 30 years is about the average age.

However, there are a few drawbacks associated with trees of a great age. One is the development of 'stag's head', a problem seen in various trees, particularly oaks. Some of the branches die, leaving them bare and stripped of bark – supposedly resembling antlers.

In some cases, this makes the tree look attractively aged, while in others it will simply look diseased and unsightly. Although the tree is usually very healthy, these branches can be removed to return the tree to its normal appearance.

Another problem is that the branches may start to sag and fall away. A similar and more frequent occurrence is when the trunks of multi-stemmed trees start to fall apart. These susceptible branches can be braced if the tree is an important one. This is best left to the professionals, as an inadequately braced tree may fall at a later date, damaging the tree and possibly injuring passers-by.

Felling small trees

Trees unfortunately need to be felled from time to time, whether because they are growing in the wrong place – such as too near a building – or because they are dying. For large, well-established trees it is usually best left to the experts, but some amateur gardeners will be able to cope with felling small trees.

Assessing the task

Generally, felling trees is a job for the expert. Even if the way is clear in the garden, it is still a skilled job to get the tree to drop exactly where required, and if it is growing among other trees or shrubs, or stands near fences or buildings, it may need to be taken down branch by branch, which involves quite a lot of clambering around in the tree.

Apart from the skills this requires, there is also the question of equipment. Not many gardeners have chainsaws capable of dealing with a tree and, although you can hire them, they are tools that have to be handled with caution and expertise.

Professional tree surgeons specialize in doing this type of work and they should know precisely how to get the tree down without damaging the property or themselves. There is also the question of what you will do with the wood afterwards, whereas tree surgeons will dispose of it for you. If they shred the wood and leaves, you could ask them to leave it for you to turn into compost or to use as a mulch.

One tree has fallen into another and it will be a difficult job, involving climbing into the tree canopy, to get it down safely.

What can you tackle?

If you feel sufficiently confident, you may be able to tackle a small tree, especially a multi-stemmed one that is not too tall or heavy, yourself. Before cutting, ensure that the ground is clear and that you have an exit plan for a quick getaway if things should go wrong. It is important that you establish the lean of the tree to ensure that it falls where you want it to. Trees are large, heavy objects, especially when horizontal, so take care that you have enough space.

For a clear fell, cut a notch on the side in the direction you want the tree to fall and then cut through from the other side level with this notch. The tree will start to topple in the right direction just before the trunk is cut through. Once it is down, dig up the remaining stump. This is a tough job.

Employing professional arborists

Always ensure that you are employing people who have been properly trained and belong to a professional association. It is also important to check that they are fully insured. Avoid using anyone who knocks on your door to offer to chop trees down as such people are rarely skilled enough to do the job properly and, if anything goes wrong, you could be faced with a very large compensation bill.

FELLING A SMALL TREE

1 Small trees, such as this birch, that are situated in a clear space may well be within the capabilities of most gardeners, but do not tackle the job if you have any doubts at all.

2 Start by making a sloping cut at 45 degrees on the side of the tree that is facing the direction in which you want it to fall. Saw into the tree by between a quarter and one-third.

3 Follow this initial cut with a horizontal cut just below it, so that the two cuts eventually meet, cutting out a wedge in the side of the trunk.

4 Remove the wedge from the trunk. This should ensure that when the tree is cut through, it will fall on the side where you have cut the wedge.

5 Start sawing on the other side of the tree opposite the horizontal cut. As the saw nears the removed wedge of wood, the tree will begin to fall forward.

6 Step back quickly as the tree falls, just in case it springs back as it hits the ground. Remove the remaining stump or cut it flush to the ground and leave it there to rot.

Renovation pruning

If you take over an old garden when you buy a new house, you may well find that any older trees or those that have been neglected for many years will require renovation pruning.

When to renovate?

Trees take a long time to grow to maturity and will leave a large gap if removed. If at all possible, it is best to try and bring them back to their former glory.

There may also be preservation orders on the trees, so it might be illegal to remove or prune them without permission. It could even be illegal to carry out major renovation work without permission, so it is always best to check with local authorities before you begin work on an old tree.

Pruning steps

Your aim with neglected trees is to turn back the clock and perform all the tasks that should have been carried out in previous years. The best time to rejuvenate is in the late autumn or early winter.

Tree renovation times

Mid- to late winter (before growth starts)
Acer spp. (maple)
Aesculus spp. (horse chestnut)
Betula spp. (birch)
Conifers
Juglans spp. (walnut)
Salix spp. (willow)

Any season, apart from spring
Carpinus (hornbeam)
Fagus spp. (beech)
Quercus spp. (oak)
Tilia spp. (lime)

Early summer
Cornus spp. (dogwood)
Ornamental plums and cherries

RENOVATING AN OVERGROWN TREE

1 Some trees, such as this contorted hazel, can become overgrown and need to be carefully renovated to bring back their shape and interest.

2 Start the renovation by removing all the dead and damaged wood. This will allow you to see what remains much more clearly.

3 Thin out some of the branches in order to remove the congestion, especially towards the middle of the tree. Remove old and weak growths first.

4 The dead stub reveals how poor pruning can cause die-back, as the previous cut was made too high. Cut back tightly, as shown here.

Start, as always, by removing any dead, diseased and damaged wood. This should remove quite a bit of material and allow you to begin to see the structure of a tree.

Next, remove any water or epicormic shoots along with any weak growths, especially those that have developed in the centre of the tree. Where branches cross over or rub, cut them out. The tree should now begin to show its true shape.

Step back and examine the tree closely to determine whether there is any overcrowding and whether any other branches require removal.

Overgrown trees, like this *Malus* (crab apple), will inevitably contain a lot of dead or damaged wood. This should be one of the first things to be removed during renovation pruning as it will allow you to assess the extent to which further pruning is required.

Any crossed and rubbing branches should also be carefully removed during renovation pruning. Use a proper pruning saw to cut thicker branches and wear gloves and suitable clothing.

Also, check if the previous owner has merely pruned the outside of the tree, removing the new extension growth on the tips of the branches, so that it has thickened up around the perimeter, looking rather hedge-like. You will have to reduce and thin this growth drastically to bring the tree back to something resembling a normal appearance.

Not all trees like to be pruned hard all in one go. In some cases, it can kill them. It is usually better to prune them over a number of years, taking out just a bit at a time. This means that the tree will look untidy over this period, but it should benefit by your patience.

Aftercare

Renovation is a drastic treatment for any tree, so ensure that it is fed and kept well watered during any dry spells the following summer so that it can recover properly. Mulching will help to preserve the moisure in the soil around the tree roots, where it is most needed.

Over time, weeping trees can develop a congested habit, as shown by the crown of this tree. Thinning out and formative pruning should be carried out in winter.

Pollarding and coppicing

The traditional techniques of pollarding and coppicing have been of value, both economically and aesthetically, for many centuries. While less common now as a means of harvesting wood, both are still used to control the size and shape of trees.

Landscaping and conservation

Today, pollarding and coppicing have largely dropped out of use as a rural industry, and in the countryside are mainly done for landscaping and conservation reasons. However, in urban areas, trees often require pollarding to prevent them from outgrowing their allotted space, casting shade and obstructing utility wires, cables and street lighting.

Pollards that have not been cut for many years will have top-heavy crowns and re-pollarding them should only be done by experts. Unfortunately, a pollarded tree looks rather ugly in a garden, but the work may be necessary in order to avoid the possibility of bad weather or structural weakness causing branches to fall.

Pollarding

This technique involves cutting back the heads of main branches, or cutting off all the branches to leave only the main stem. This results in a profusion of new shoots being produced at the ends of the framework branches, or from the top of the trunks, the following year. Every three to four years these shoots are removed back to exactly the same points.

Pollarding has been undertaken for many centuries to manipulate the shape and height of trees, and it is a successful way of controlling a tree's height and spread, because the tree becomes accustomed to having its foliage removed regularly.

The technique was also often practised in order to produce repeated crops of small-sized wood growing out of reach of hungry deer and livestock. The wood produced could be used in a number of ways – oaks and sweet chestnuts were popular choices for contstruction and firewood – and the shoots and foliage were cut for additional animal fodder.

Willows are often pollarded not only to keep them contained, but also to show off their vibrant, beautiful and colourful young stems.

This tree has been regularly pollarded; the branches are rising from the top of the trunk.

POLLARDING A TREE

1 Remove all the branches, using either a pair of strong long-handled pruners or a saw. At this stage, it doesn't matter if some of the stubs are a bit long.

2 Tidy up the pruned cuts by sawing through the base of each of the branches. The new shoots will eventually appear around the edge of these cuts.

Pollarding prolongs a tree's life and, if carried out regularly, pollarded trees can survive for centuries.

Coppicing

This is the ancient art of cutting back all the main shoots of a multi-stemmed tree almost to ground level to promote vigorous regrowth and provide a sustainable supply of timber. These then regenerate and another set of main shoots develops, only for these to be removed as well.

Trees and shrubs that are cut down this way can produce shoots that grow over 30cm (12in) in a week, and a coppiced tree may live many times longer than if the tree had not been coppiced.

For example, willow is often coppiced annually, to produce thin, flexible stems that are used for weaving – in the past these were in great demand for making baskets and fencing, and these skills are still practised. To obtain large, strong poles, *Castanea sativa* (sweet chestnut) can be coppiced on a 14-year cycle.

Many broad-leaved trees, particularly *Corylus* (hazel), can be cut right down to the stump. In the case of hazel, the poles are harvested approximately every eight years.

For the gardener, it can be an interesting experience growing the poles, which have many uses in the garden, depending on the size at which they are cut. Other trees, such as *Catalpa* (bean tree) and *Paulownia* (coffin tree), can be coppiced annually to produce large, lustrous leaves.

How to coppice

Grow the tree as a multi-stemmed form. Once the stems have reached the required size, cut them off near to the base with a saw, between late winter and early spring. The cuts should be slightly sloped to allow rainwater to run off.

In subsequent years, new shoots will appear and the cycle of growth and coppicing can be repeated. Prune out the weakest shoots to ensure only the strongest grow, and to allow equal spacing between the shoots.

Hazel can be coppiced back to a low framework of branches. This will promote the growth of many straight stems, which can be cut regularly.

Pruning conifers

Conifers are very popular trees, forming an architectural backbone to the garden that varies little from season to season. They are also relatively easy to grow, require little attention once they have been planted and their foliage appears in myriad colours.

Different treatment

Unfortunately, many gardeners do not realize that conifers must be treated differently to their deciduous relatives. As a result, it is not unusual to see a row of dead coniferous trees in a garden where the owner has decided that the trees have grown too large and so has lopped off half of each tree – only to discover that the foliage does not grow back.

Cutting into old wood

Most conifers are reluctant to put out new shoots from old wood, so only cut back into the new growth. Cutting back into the older wood creates a bald patch, and removing too much can kill the tree.

If you want to control the height, either ensure that the tree you buy will reach only to the height you want, or be prepared to clip in once or twice a year, removing only some of the new growth.

How to prune

Most conifers produce resinous sap that bleeds freely from the stems if they are cut while the tree is in active growth. For this reason, pruning is best carried out from autumn to midwinter.

If you need to limit the size of the tree, clip it lightly every year, keeping the natural shape as far as possible. This can be quite effective, but it takes some skill to achieve a really natural look. As always, any dead, dying or diseased wood should be cut out, preferably as far back as possible. You should also remove any

TRAINING A YOUNG CONIFER

Most conifers are better left to grow unchecked, but you can alter their shape successfully if you begin when they are young and avoid cutting into old wood.

YEAR ONE To create a bare trunk, remove the bottom branches, as well as any crossing or dead branches.

SUBSEQUENT YEARS Continue to remove any crossing or dead branches, as well as any new growth low down on the trunk.

Young conifers rarely need any training, and will form a pleasing shape if they are allowed to grow naturally.

odd growths that stick out beyond the shape required. Do not leave these for too long, or they may grow too vigorously and leave a hole where you removed them.

Similarly, on variegated forms, there may be some reversion to plain green leaves and this needs to be removed or it will gradually outgrow the variegation.

Conifers that have a strong vertical habit display a characteristic known as central leader dominance. A single stem, ending in a terminal bud, grows upwards and thickens to form a solid trunk. Sometimes, as a result of damage, two leaders form. It is essential to remove one or the tree will not develop its characteristic shape and the fork of the trunk will be a weak point that is prone to further damage.

Pruning conifers

Most conifers will stand a little light pruning as long as you restrict yourself to the new growth. In general, this will apply only if you are cutting the tree to a shape, as in topiary, or creating a hedge. If done every year, this will help to restrict the size. However, once a conifer has reached maturity, there is little that can be done to reduce its size, except for the following examples:

Cephalotaxus *Sequoia*
Cryptomeria *Taxus*
Cunninghamia *Torreya*

These will tolerate being cut back into old wood. One of the most common garden conifers, the Lawson cypress (*Chamaecyparis lawsoniana*), will not break from old wood, so do not attempt to prune it except for a light trim to retain its size and shape. Young conifers can have their side shoots pinched out to produce bushier growth and a denser branching habit.

PRUNING TECHNIQUES FOR CONIFERS

1 If you need to prune a conifer, cut the shoots well back into the tree, so they don't show.

2 Dead wood spoils the appearance of the conifer, so remove it and wait for new growth to fill in the gaps.

3 Conifers do not need much pruning, but new growth can be clipped back to restrict the size of the tree. Do not cut into old wood.

4 If you shear the conifer, you will cut some of its leaves in half. Instead, pinch out the growing tips to restrict growth.

Tying in

As tight-growing trees get old and large, snow and sometimes wind can pull a branch out of place so that it sticks out sideways. This is a problem for shaped trees that have several main stems or near-vertical branches. If removed, these will leave a large gap that is unlikely to be refilled with new shoots. The only solution is to pull them back into position and tie them in place.

If large branches are involved, you may need professional help. If the tree is distorted badly, it may be advisable to start again with a new tree. A conifer in such a poor state is very difficult to renovate and can look very ugly if left as it is. It is also common practice to wire hoops around the branches to encourage a more conical shape. These are periodically removed and replaced if the wire starts to damage the branches.

Pruning palms

Palm trees require little pruning except for the cosmetic removal of old leaves when they die. Additional cosmetic work can be undertaken to remove the fibrous material that builds up on trunks.

Buta capitata (Pindo or jelly palm) is grown for its architectural arching branches. Like most palms, it requires little pruning apart from the removal of spent flower trusses and dead leaves.

Smart palms

In an attempt to make your palm tree look smart at all times, you could be in danger of over-pruning, which could weaken or even kill it. Just like other trees, palms need an adequate number of fronds to process enough energy to develop and flower. As this cycle goes on, the older fronds die off naturally. At this point they can be safely removed from the tree to tidy it up.

Many people mistakenly believe that palms should be pruned in order to reduce the danger of damage by strong winds. In fact, the flexible leaves and trunks, and low wind-resistance, of palms make them nearly storm-proof. Despite this, in many coastal areas it is common practice to remove all but the top tier of leaves each year just before the hurricane season – the technique is known as hurricane pruning. Though unneccessary, the practice does not seriously harm the trees as long as enough green leaves are left each time it is carried out.

Pruning palms

The older, dying fronds should be pruned off close to the base of the stem, but care should be taken to ensure that the main trunk and crown are not damaged. A short section of the leaf stalk should be left intact and allowed to fall naturally or removed the following year.

Removal of dead leaves can be undertaken at any time of the year, although it is best done during late spring, once the palm tree is actively growing, so that any wounds can heal quickly. In warmer climates, where the risk of cross-infection from diseases spreading from pruning cuts is higher, equipment should be sterilized when moving from tree to tree. A good-quality household disinfectant can be used to clean any pruning equipment.

However, leaving the dead leaves presents no health risk to the palm as in their natural habitats the dead fronds would remain attached and develop into dead 'skirts' that may extend down the trunk of the palm and can provide useful habitats for insects and birds. However, this is often considered unsightly and an uncluttered stem with the dead leaves removed is the usual option.

Green leaves can be removed, but care should be taken not to rip or tear off the leaves as this will scar the trunk and increase the risk of infection. If you do need to remove a green frond, don't remove those

Palm pest problems

There are a number of caterpillars, bark boring beetles and weevils that affect palm trees and most of these cause physical damage to the leaves or stems which can make them look unsightly, but will seldom kill the palm tree.

However, there are also a number of soil-borne organisms, such as bud rot, which kills the crown of the palm, and fusarium wilt, which causes yellowing and eventual death of the fronds, and once infected there is no real cure.

Ganoderma butt root is a disease that rots the base of palms, causes the stem to die, makes the palm structurally unsound, and rots out the trunk. Finally, lethal yellowing disease causes the palm fronds to turn yellow and droop, beginning on the lower leaves and spreading throughout the crown of the palm, and causes all the fronds to die.

Treatment is expensive as the disease is not fully understood although it is believed it is caused by a bacterium-like organism and spread by insects. Infected trees should be removed and destroyed to stop the spread.

growing horizontally or upward. Remove only the downward-growing ones, as these would naturally be shed in the future.

Aftercare for palms

Although palms are relatively trouble-free landscape plants, they may succumb to a number of ailments. In cooler climates, winter damage on palms depends on the lowest temperature and the duration of cold. Cold damage appears first in the foliage and causes the leaves to turn brown and die. Although the foliage may die completely, as long as the root system and crown of the palm survives then the damage may only be superficial. However, if the root system freezes, the palm will not recover.

The roots will often tolerate temperatures several degrees cooler than the leaves, so even if the foliage dies there is still a chance that the palm will re-sprout when the temperatures warm in spring. Any damaged foliage should be trimmed before the emergence of new leaves in spring.

In subtropical and tropical climates, many of the problems associated with palms are caused by compacted nutrient-deficient soils that place the palm under stress and make it less likely to be able to ward off pests and diseases. For this reason, you should make every effort to provide the correct soil conditions for your particular palm. Soil aeration and foliar feeding may overcome short-term problems.

Bismarckia nobilis is a stunning tropical palm, and the ones shown here are excellent specimens, with clear trunks and balanced heads of leaves.

Pruning fruit trees

All fruit trees require pruning to ensure that they continue to produce fruit. Some require twice yearly pruning while others need considerably less.

Training and pruning cordons

Cordons have a single stem trained at an angle of 45 degrees. After planting at the correct angle, tie a bamboo cane behind the main stem and to the top wire. Prune side shoots to just above the third bud.

In the first summer, tie extension growth to the cane and prune back any new shoots from the main stem to above the third bud. Prune new shoots produced from the stubs of the side shoots produced the previous year to their first leaf.

Each winter afterwards, cut back the main stem's new growth to within 15cm (6in). Once the tree reaches the top of its support, cut any extension growth to the first bud.

The pole-grown apples above have been grown as vertical cordons. The bottoms of the trunks have been protected against rabbit attack with wire guards.

These pears have been grown in a cordon against a trellis, which is a method suitable for small gardens. Cordons provide height, rather than the spread achieved with a fan.

Each summer, prune new shoots produced from the stubs that were cut back the previous year to the first leaf.

Training and pruning fan trees

Fan-trained trees have up to ten equally spaced ribs radiating from the main stem. It is a good way of training fruit trees because it produces a large number of fruit-bearing stems. Use five to seven parallel wires, about 30cm (12in) apart. Pull them taut and held 10–15cm (4–6in) away from the wall. The bottom wire should be about 45cm (18in) above ground-level. For a free-standing fan, the posts must be solidly set in the ground, 2–2.5m (6–8ft) apart.

PRUNING AN ESTABLISHED APPLE CORDON

1 Established cordon apples against a fence. They take up very little space and enable the gardener to grow several different varieties.

2 In the winter, prune back any new side shoots to one or two buds.

3 New growth on existing side shoots should also be cut back to one or two buds in the winter.

4 In summer, cut back the main leader once it has reached the top support. Do this every summer, cutting back to one or two buds.

5 In summer, you should also cut back any new shoots to two or three leaves.

6 Any new shoots on existing side shoots should be cut back to one leaf.

Buy a feathered tree that has two strong shoots just below the proposed position of the bottom wire. Cut off the leader just above the upper of these two. Tie the laterals to canes, then attach these to the wires at an angle of 40 degrees. Shorten the shoots to about 45cm (18in) to a bud on the underside. This will stimulate the production of side shoots later that year. Tie these in to new canes as they develop.

The top bud will produce a new leader for each of the main arms. Tie this in along the cane in the same direction. Cut out any unwanted shoots, keeping both sides balanced. Remove new growth from the main trunk. Cut back the tips of laterals on either side of the main stems.

Remove any growth that projects from the fan. Over the next three years, allow the fan to develop so that it branches more towards the periphery and covers the space evenly.

Training and pruning espaliers

Espalier trees have three or four horizontal tiers of branches trained along the supporting wires. Follow the method described for pruning fans, except that the main stem should be pruned back to just above the horizontal wire, and the side shoots should be trained along canes held at 45 degrees in their first year, then lowered to the horizontal wire in their second.

Each summer, all unwanted new shoots should be pruned to the first leaf and suitably placed new shoots should be tied in to the next pair of canes. Once the tree covers the support, cut back the extension growth of the main stem to one bud above the top wire and treat each branch following the technique described for a cordon.

TRAINING AN APPLE FAN

Fans, like most decorative forms of apple, need a lot of care and attention in order to prevent them from becoming overgrown and out of hand. An apple trained in this way will need attention both in the summer and in the winter.

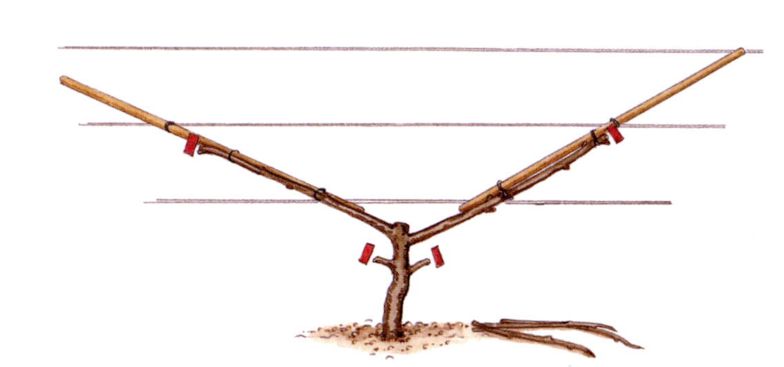

YEAR ONE, WINTER Start with a feathered tree which is planted in winter. Cut off the leader just below the bottom wire and tie in two laterals to canes attached to the wires at 40 degrees. Cut these back to about 45cm (18in). Shorten any other remaining laterals to a couple of buds.

YEAR ONE, SUMMER In the following summer tie in the side shoots that develop on the laterals to form an even spread of branches, but remove any that crowd the space. Now remove any side shoots that you cut back in the winter from the main trunk.

SUBSEQUENT YEARS, SUMMER Continue to tie in the developing side shoots so that a fan-like framework of branches is developed. Cut out their tips so that they continue to branch. Cut back any unwanted shoots to two or three leaves to create fruiting spurs.

Apple trees

As a general rule, apple trees are pruned to encourage new shoots that bear fruit and remove any surplus wood. However, if the tree is left unpruned, its growth will become congested. This in turn causes poorer fruit production because less light is able to enter the canopy, preventing the tree from bearing as many flowers as it should and stopping the fruit from ripening.

Pruning is usually carried out once the tree has become dormant during late autumn and winter. The aim is to achieve an open shape with a good framework of about five main branches. This will allow light into the canopy. In order to do this you will need to remove any weak, damaged, dead or diseased wood, and epicormic shoots.

What is the difference between espalier and cordon trees?

Cordons are single-stemmed trees that are planted at an angle of 45 degrees and supported by wirework. Any side branches are pruned away. Cordons crop earlier than most other forms and take up less space, allowing more varieties to grow.

Growing fruit trees as espaliers is a technique of training trees by pruning them to create formal, two-dimensional patterns with the branches of the tree. The technique was popular many centuries ago and was used to decorate walls. When trees are grown as an espalier against a sunny wall, they receive almost as much sunlight as a regular tree, despite being smaller. The wall will reflect the sunlight, as well as providing shelter and storing warmth from the sun. These factors allow espalier-grown fruit trees to succeed in cooler climates. They also allow the fruit to ripen more quickly.

With older trees, fruit quality and yield diminishes significantly so some quite heavy pruning will need to be carried out in order to increase the tree's productivity and get it back into shape.

If the tree has become too large for its space and casts too much shadow over the garden, you should cut back the top portion to the lateral branches.

Spur- and tip-bearers

Having achieved a sound, basic framework that allows adequate light to reach the canopy, attention now needs to be given to the rest of the tree. The method used depends on whether the tree is spur-bearing or tip-bearing.

Spur-bearing trees, which are the most common type of apple tree, bear most of their fruit on older wood. Tip-bearing trees, on the other hand, produce most of their fruit buds at the tips of slender young shoots that have grown during the previous summer.

For spur-bearing apple trees, remove any overly vigorous and unwanted wood, as well as any branches that are crossing or rubbing. The leaders of all the previous season's growth can then be reduced by about a quarter to one-third. If any of the spurs are overcrowded, remove the older and less productive wood.

For tip-bearing apple trees, you can either leave the young wood unpruned or just cut the tip back to the first strong bud. Take out the older shoots back to a young shoots to ensure renewal and continued fruiting. Having done this, carefully take out any crossing and rubbing branches, along with any branches that are too vigorous or that are misplaced.

Plums are ready for picking when they are slightly soft to the touch. You can usually tell by their colour, too. Once they are ripe they should be easy to remove from the tree.

Thinning the crop

Though it seems wasteful, it is necessary to reduce the fruit to one apple per cluster. This will actually result in a better crop, since it is seed production, rather than the juicy flesh, that takes most of the tree's energy – the fewer the fruits, the larger they will be. They will also receive better exposure to the sun. This also applies to pear trees.

Pear trees

Generally, pear trees are more upright than apple trees, but the pruning techniques are very similar. It is usual to prune pear trees during the winter.

Once the tree is established, the tree will not grow in a particularly vigorous way, so pruning is restricted to just thinning the spurs. However, you should remove any over-vigorous and unwanted wood, along with any branches that cross or rub against each other.

If the leaders are over-long, reduce them by about a quarter to one-third of the previous season's growth. Check the spurs: any that are overcrowded should have their older and less productive wood removed.

Plum and cherry trees

Once the basic shape of the tree has been established, cherry and plum trees need little pruning apart from the removal of dead, diseased or congested growth as well as any weak or crossing wood.

Plum trees should be pruned during the summer in order to prevent them from getting silver leaf disease and canker. Sour cherries are produced on one-year-old wood and should be pruned after the fruit has been harvested. Cut back about one-third of the fruiting stems to the first new shoot lower down the stem.

Plum and sweet cherry trees produce most of their fruit at the base of one-year-old and older shoots. This means that they are not suitable for training as cordons or espaliers but can be trained as fans, bushes or pyramids.

After formative pruning of a fan-trained tree has established the framework, you need to ensure that there is a constant supply of new growth. In summer, cut back all shoots that have fruited to a new shoot lower down. Tie this in to the supporting cane and prune out any unwanted growth to maintain the shape.

Harvesting fruit and storing gluts

Pick the fruit as soon as it is ripe. You can pick plums when they are slightly under-ripe and store them in the refrigerator for a couple of weeks. Sweet cherries do not continue to mature after picking so do not harvest them until they are ready. Ripe fruit is best eaten straight away, although it will last a few days if kept somewhere cool. Gluts of fruit can be made into jams and preserves. Plums and sweet cherries can be frozen after they have been split to remove the stone (pit).

TRAINING A PLUM DWARF PYRAMID

Some varieties of plum lend themselves to being grown on a dwarfing stock and can be grown as dwarf pyramids. Check that you buy a suitable variety. These are particularly useful in a small garden where just a small quantity of plums is required. Because of their small size it may be possible to grow several varieties of plum as pyramids in a small area.

YEAR ONE, WINTER Plant a feathered tree in winter. In early spring, cut out its leader at about 1.5m (5ft) from the ground. Cut out all the side shoots below about 45cm (18in) and then reduce all remaining laterals by about half.

YEAR ONE, SUMMER The following midsummer you will need to cut back the new growth on the main branches to about 20cm (8in) to an outward-facing bud. You should also cut back all the sub-laterals to around 15cm (6in).

YEAR TWO, SPRING In the second spring cut back the new growth made by the leader by about two-thirds. No other pruning is required at this time of the year.

ESTABLISHED PRUNING, SUMMER The tree may be mature by the third or fourth spring. Once mature, cut back any vigorous growth to a few leaves in summer, and remove any dead, diseased or damaged wood and thin out any congested areas by taking out older wood.

Propagating trees

Most gardeners with an average-sized plot will have room for only a small number of trees, and will usually prefer to buy ready-grown trees rather than wait for them to grow from seeds or cuttings. However, some people choose to propagate trees simply because they find the process fascinating and rewarding in itself, though some methods require specialist equipment.

Seed propagation is the easiest method of growing new trees, as long as you remember some basic rules and are prepared to accept that the seedling trees may not be identical to the parent tree, and might even be hybrids. Many tree seeds also require special treatment to help them overcome dormancy.

Propagating trees by asexual (or vegetative) 'cloning' methods such as cuttings, grafting or layering is the only sure way to guarantee that the offspring will be identical to their parents, as they will be clones. However, the more sophisticated the method, the more sophisticated the equipment and facilities required, and the more skill needed by the propagator.

Saving seeds is by far the easiest method of propagation as it requires little specialist equipment.

Propagating from seed

Growing trees from seeds at home is similar to growing any other garden plants. However, if you collect the seed yourself, the resulting plant may vary from the tree from which the seed came. Alternatively, you can buy seed, which is more likely to come true to type and match the parent tree. However, some commercial seed may have been collected from wild plants and will not necessarily come true, as many trees hybridize in the wild.

Fleshy fruit would normally be eaten by birds and animals and digested, so you need to ensure that you reproduce similar conditions for them to germinate.

Collecting seed

For trees that will be grown outdoors it is sensible to obtain seed only from species that will grow in your garden. It would be pointless, for example, to collect tree seed in Hawaii and expect it to grow outside in Canada. Seed collected in the south of a temperate country might grow in the north, but the tree might come into leaf so early that it will be killed by spring frosts.

Collect seed from trees that are healthy and have the qualities you want, such as good leaf colour, attractive habit, hardiness and disease resistance. Many countries do not permit the importation of unlicensed plant material, so check before you collect seeds abroad, or you may lose them at customs.

Tamarind pods grow up to 18cm (7in) long and contain a soft, edible pulp.

Most seed should be collected when it is ripe. Some seed, such as *Acer*, has a natural inhibitor to prevent it from germinating too soon, so collect it before it is fully ripe. If you are collecting from conifers spread out the unopened cones on a sheet of paper in a well-ventilated, warm room until the scales open. Shake the cones to release the seed. Some pines, such as *Pinus coulteri* (big-cone pine), require high temperatures to release the seeds, and should be placed near a fire to open.

The seeds contained within fleshy fruits, such as those of *Sorbus* (mountain ash) and *Crataegus* (hawthorn), are released by mashing the fruit to a pulp, then floating the remains in water to separate the seeds from the pulp. These seeds often require a period of fermentation to mimic the passage through a bird's digestive system before they will germinate, so keep them in warm water for a few days.

Dry fruit, such as that from *Betula* (birch), *Catalpa* (bean tree) and *Stewartia*, can be spread thinly on a sheet of paper in a warm, well-ventilated room. The fruit will split and the seeds can be collected.

Seed dormancy

Without a proper period of dormancy, seeds might germinate in the middle of winter and the young plants would be killed by cold. The length and type of dormancy varies from species to species. Ripened seed of *Ulmus* spp. (elm), *Populus* spp. (poplar) and *Pinus sylvestris* (Scots pine) shows little dormancy and germinates easily. The seed of *Acer* spp. (maple), *Fraxinus* spp. (ash), *Liquidambar* and *Sorbus* (mountain ash) requires a cold period (similar in duration and temperature to winter) followed by a period of warmth (to imitate spring) to germinate.

EXTRACTING SEED FROM FLESHY BERRIES

1 Cut a spray of ripe berries from the tree (shown here are rowan berries) and squash individual fruits to release the seed.

2 Wash the seed in lukewarm water, rubbing it gently, and leave in a warm place to soak for a few days.

3 Dry the seed on an absorbent paper towel. The seed is then ready for sowing in pots or seed trays.

Seed dormancy

When tree seed does not readily germinate following ripening, it is probably waiting for the right treatment to 'break' its dormancy. Dormancy is the mechanism that prevents seed from germinating until the conditions are right for the young tree to grow successfully.

The dormancy of many species can be overcome by sowing the seed in containers, placing them outside and letting nature run its course. Seed bought in spring should be placed in some compost (soil mix) in a plastic bag and stored in a refrigerator for six weeks, before being moved to a warm place, such as an airing cupboard. The seed can then be sown into a container and allowed to germinate.

Sow seed thinly on the surface of a container filled with a suitable growing medium such as seed compost (soil mix). Do not cover fine seed. Larger seed should be covered by about 2.5cm (1in) of sieved compost. Carefully label the containers before placing them in a greenhouse or cold frame or on a sunny window ledge.

After the seed has germinated and when two true leaves have grown (palms are monocots and have just one true leaf), the seedlings can be carefully transplanted to larger containers and grown on.

SOWING SEED

1 Prepare pots or seed trays of seed compost (soil mix). Water the compost well and allow the water to drain. The compost should be moist but not sodden. Lightly place the seed on the surface.

2 Gently press the seed into the compost. The seed should be covered to its own depth with compost. Very fine seeds should be surface sown.

3 Lightly topdress the container with grit and place in a cold frame or in a cool, sheltered spot outdoors.

Propagating from cuttings

Trees are generally more difficult than shrubs to grow from cuttings because the wood is older and less likely to root without special facilities and equipment. Despite this, there are some species that can be propagated successfully from stem tip, softwood and hardwood cuttings.

Stem tip cuttings

Propagation by cutting, a vegetative process, differs from growing from seed because the cuttings will produce plants that are identical to the parent plants. Some species of tree, such as *Quercus* spp. (oak), are difficult to root from cuttings, but conifers, *Ilex* spp. (holly) and *Catalpa* spp. (bean tree) are generally easier, as are some maples.

Stem tip cuttings are the most widely used method of propagation. Softwood cuttings of deciduous trees should be collected in early summer and will require moist, humid conditions, such as those found in a propagator, to prevent them from wilting before they root. Conifers are propagated from more ripened wood, so take material for cuttings in late autumn.

Taking softwood cuttings

Cut a terminal tip about 15cm (6in) long, cutting just below a leaf node, and remove the lower leaves so that there are leaves on the top two-thirds of the cutting. Remove any flowerbuds or seedpods.

Fill a container with a suitable rooting medium, such as equal quantities of peat and sand, peat and perlite, or coir and perlite. Dip the base of the cutting in a hormone rooting compound, shaking off the excess, use a stick or dibber to make a hole in the compost (soil mix) and insert the cutting so that it stands up. Make sure that the leaves do not touch the compost. Cut large leaves in half to reduce water loss.

Laurus nobilis (bay) is suitable for propagation by stem tip cutting, which should be taken from the parent tree in spring.

Rooting hormones

You can increase your chances of success with most stem cuttings, particularly those that are reluctant to root, by using a rooting hormone. When applied to the cut surface at the base of the cutting, the hormone encourages root formation and increases the speed of rooting. Rooting hormones are usually formulated as powders, but you may also come across liquids and gels.

To avoid contaminating the hormone, tip a small amount into a saucer. Dip the cutting's cut end into the hormone, shaking off excess if you use powder, and insert into the compost (soil mix). After treating the batch of cuttings, discard any powder that is left over in the saucer. Rooting hormone deteriorates rapidly, so buy fresh stock every year to make sure of its effectiveness.

Holly is easier to root from semi-ripe stem cuttings than many other species of tree.

TAKING TIP CUTTINGS OF EVERGREEN AND DECIDUOUS TREES

1 Take cuttings from the tree you want to propagate, just above a leaf joint. *Laurus nobilis* (bay) is shown here.

2 Trim each cutting at the base below a leaf joint. The cutting should be about 10–15cm (4–6in) long.

3 Remove the lower leaves to expose a clear length of stem.

4 On evergreen trees, to accelerate rooting, pare away a sliver of bark 2.5cm (1in) long at the base of the cutting. Dip in rooting hormone.

5 Insert the cutting into a pot of compost (soil mix) using a dibber to make the hole. Label clearly.

6 Firm in the cutting and water well. Place in a cold frame or in a sheltered outdoor spot, ensuring that the cutting is kept humid.

Keep the cuttings moist at all times by covering the container with a polythene bag or placing it in a propagator and misting. Spraying with a fungicide will reduce the risk of mould. Any dead leaves should be removed quickly.

Check the cuttings periodically for signs of roots growing out of the bottom of the container, but remove them only when fibrous feeder roots are evident, potting them on into a proprietary potting compost. Don't forget to label the pots.

When you come to plant the cuttings outside, remember that they have been kept in a very humid environment and so will require careful acclimatization.

Trees such as this alder can be propagated from seed, soft tip cutting, hardwood cutting or from suckers.

Propagating from hardwood cuttings

At the end of the growing season, after the leaves have fallen off the trees and the current year's growth has fully ripened, hardwood cuttings can be taken. Unlike other methods, hardwood cuttings require no special facilities.

When to take cuttings

Many deciduous trees are easily propagated from hardwood cuttings, which are taken when the tree is fully dormant and showing no obvious signs of active growth. The wood for hardwood cuttings is firm and does not bend easily. Trees propagated this way include *Cornus* (dogwood), *Salix* (willow) and *Populus* (poplar). Most will root successfully in the open ground.

Rooting occurs when the cut surface successfully undergoes a period of callusing over the winter. This then enables the roots to appear in the spring. By altering the planting depth of the cuttings, you can control whether a single-stemmed or multi-stemmed tree is produced.

Types of cutting

The three types of hardwood cuttings are straight, mallet and heel. A straight cutting is the technique most commonly used. Mallet and heel cuttings are used for plants that might otherwise be more difficult to root, such as some deciduous conifers like *Larix* spp. (larch).

For the heel cutting, a small section of older wood is included at the base of the cutting. This is because the plant produces more hormones at this point, so including it as part of the cutting means that the propagation is more likely to be successful.

For the mallet cutting, an entire section of older stem wood is included with the cutting.

How to take cuttings

To take the cuttings, cut lengths of the current season's growth, from a healthy, disease-free tree. Each stem will probably yield two or three cuttings, making this a very economical method of propagation.

Remove any flowers and flower buds when preparing cuttings so the cutting's energy can be directed towards producing new roots rather than flowers.

Hardwood cuttings will take up to a year to root. If a heavy frost lifts them, gently firm them in again, using your feet or hands. Once they have rooted, they can be grown on *in situ* for a further season or two before being transferred to their final positions in the garden.

Propagating from tree suckers

Some trees naturally produce numerous shoots that form thickets, which are called suckers. These can be separated from the parent tree by severing the roots around the sucker. Keep the plant roots moist until you are ready to plant them up. This should be done following the usual planting procedures.

Trees that produce suckers suitable for propagation include: *Populus tremula* (aspen); *Alnus* (alder); *Cornus sanguinea* (dogwood); *Ligustrum lucidum* (glossy privet); *Populus canescens* (grey poplar); *Pyrus communis* (wild pear); and *Ulmus* spp. (elms).

Cornus (dogwood) is one of the easiest types of tree to propagate by hardwood cutting, and once they have rooted they will establish and grow quite quickly.

TAKING HARDWOOD CUTTINGS

1 Choose stems that are firm and of pencil thickness. The length of the cutting will depend on the plant, but about 15cm (6in) is appropriate for most. Make a cut straight across the stem, just below a node.

2 Using a pair of secateurs (pruners), make the second cut about 15cm (6in) above the first. Make the cut above a node, but this time at an angle so that you will know which is the top and which the bottom of the cutting.

3 Although a rooting hormone is not essential, it can increase the success rate, especially with plants that are difficult to root. Moisten the bases of the cuttings in water first, then shake off excess water.

4 Dip each cutting into the hormone powder, and tap or shake off any excess. Rooting hormones are also available in liquid and gel forms, in which case you do not need to dip the cuttings in water first.

5 Make a slit trench with a spade, a little shallower than the length of the cuttings. Choose an unobtrusive and fairly sheltered spot in the garden to leave the cuttings undisturbed for a year.

6 Sprinkle some grit or coarse sand in the base of the slit if the ground is poorly drained. This will help to prevent waterlogging around the cuttings. Firm lightly to make sure there are no air pockets.

7 Insert the cuttings 8–10cm (3–4in) apart, upright against the back of the slit, leaving about 2.5–5cm (1–2in) above the ground.

8 Firm the soil around the cuttings, to eliminate any pockets of air that would cause the cuttings to dry out.

9 Water the cuttings and label. Continue to water them in dry weather, especially during the spring and summer months.

Propagating by layering

Layering is one of the easiest of all methods of propagating trees, since it mimics the way some species naturally form roots on low-growing branches that touch the ground.

Simple layering

Depending on the species, simple layering can be carried out in autumn, early winter or spring. It involves burying a still-attached branch in soil so that the tip of the stem emerges above the ground. Roots form on the buried section, and once this has happened the new plant can be detached from its parent and replanted elsewhere.

The process can be made more successful by nicking the underside of the stem to be buried and either pegging the stem down into a large container or into a hole filled with good-quality soil. Cover the portion of the layer that has been pegged to the soil with more soil and firm lightly before watering thoroughly. Water and weed as necessary during the following year, also checking that rooting is taking place. Water well in dry periods. The method is suitable for plants that have flexible, low-growing stems, such as *Amelanchier* (juneberry), *Cercis*, *Corylus* (hazel), *Magnolia*, *Parrotia* (Persian ironwood) and *Thuja* (arborvitae).

Air-layering

The straightforward technique of air-layering is more suitable for trees with upright, inflexible stems. A branch is wounded and then surrounded in a moisture-retaining wrapper such as sphagnum moss, which is further surrounded in a

SIMPLE LAYERING

1 Dig over the soil where you want to make the layer, incorporating some well rotted manure or compost.

2 Select a low stem and trim off side shoots. Bend it down until it touches the ground. Make a small slit in the stem at that point.

3 Make a hole 10cm (4in) deep, and lay the stem on it sloping the stem towards the parent plant. Secure in place using a hook.

4 Alternatively, you can secure the stem using a rock, as nature would have done if left to her own devices.

5 Regularly check if the plant has rooted. When it has, cut it off from the parent plant using secateurs. Make a clean cut.

6 You should now have an independent plant with its own root system. Pot up and grow on until it is big enough to be planted out.

HOW TO AIR-LAYER

1 Air-layering can be used to propagate plants whose stems cannot easily be lowered to ground level. Using secateurs (pruners), remove a few leaves from the point on the stem where you want to make the layer.

2 Using a sharp knife, carefully make an upward slit in the stem, about 2.5cm (1in) long, below an old leaf joint. Do not cut more than halfway through the stem, otherwise it may break.

3 Cut a piece of plastic that is large enough to wrap around the stem of the plant, making a wide sleeve with space to add a thick layer of moss. Fix the bottom a short distance below the cut with a twist-tie or adhesive tape.

4 Brush or wipe a small amount of rooting hormone compound (powder or gel) into the wound to speed rooting. Pack a small amount of sphagnum moss into the wound to keep it open. Alternatively, a small piece of wood can be inserted to ensure the cut stays open.

5 Pack plenty of damp sphagnum moss around the stem to enclose the wound, then cover with the sheet of plastic and secure at the top with another twist-tie or tape. Make sure that the moss is kept moist, and carefully check for roots after a month or so. When well rooted, sever from the parent to pot up.

moisture barrier such as black plastic film. Rooting hormone is often applied to encourage the wounded region to grow roots.

A branch that gets sun will root better. Use only upright branches and select an area on the branch that will allow you to cut below the future rootball so the new feeder roots will be at the top of the container to be potted in.

Two methods of injuring the branch can be used. The first method consists of removing a 1–2.5cm (½–1in) ring of bark from the branch by making two circular cuts. After removing the bark, expose the wood to be sure that the cambium layer (the light green area immediately beneath the bark) is removed to prevent bark formation and allow the roots to develop.

With the second method, a long slanting upward cut is made about ½–1cm (¼–½in) through the stem and the incision is kept open by inserting a small chip of wood. This method is used on plants where the bark does not peel off easily. Plants that are commonly air-layered include Japanese maples, figs, magnolias, mangoes, olives, loquats and many conifers.

Dusting the wound with a rooting hormone will assist rooting on some hard-to-root trees such as figs. After removing the bark or making the cut, enclose the injured area in a ball of moist sphagnum moss as soon as possible, to avoid contamination. Make sure you squeeze out excess moisture before applying the moss to the cut surface, otherwise the wood might rot.

When sufficient roots have grown from the wound, the stem from the parent plant should be removed below the wounded area. The stem can then be labelled, potted up and grown on.

Japanese maples are difficult to propagate from cuttings, but they can be produced by air-layering.

Propagation by grafting and budding

Some trees are too slow or too difficult to grow and establish when they are propagated from seed or cuttings. In these cases, they are propagated by grafting or budding. Both methods have their limitations and require specialized tools and techniques as well as an understanding of the aftercare needed.

Grafting technique

The technique that involves the uniting of two plants is called grafting. The plant to be propagated is called the scion, and it is grown on the rootstock of a compatible species, which is selected because it is readily available and more vigorous than the scion, or has some other quality, such as size or disease resistance, that the scion lacks. The scion material must be dormant, and the rootstock must be held back but ready for growth if the union is to be successful. The two plants being united must also be related: you cannot graft a *Morus* (mulberry tree) on a *Ficus* (fig tree), but you can graft *Acer platanoides* (Norway maple) on *A. rubrum* (red maple).

Budding technique

A form of grafting that is often used with fruit trees, budding involves inserting a well-developed bud from one tree under the bark of another.

The timing of both techniques is crucial, but they are rewarding methods. They can be carried out only at very specific times when weather conditions and the physiological stage of plant growth are both optimum. The timing depends on the species and the technique used.

Most selected varieties of *Sorbus aucuparia* (mountain ash) are winter grafted on to seedling grown rootstocks of *Sorbus* spp. However, in recent years budding has been more widely used.

Grafted trees are easily recognized by the grafting union near the base of the stem.

PROPAGATION BY BUDDING

1 Select good bud wood that is true to type and free from obvious damage from pests or diseases. If you are doing this in the summer, you must first remove the leaves.

2 Remove the bud from the stem using a very sharp knife. Cut out the bud with a thin shaving of the wood below the bark and leave a 'V' shape at the base.

3 Prepare the stock plant that you are going to graft on to by carefully cutting a notch from its stem that is exactly the same thickness as the bottom end of the chipped bud.

4 Place the bud into the notch, fitting the 'V'-shaped base into the notch at the base of the other cut snugly, with the cut edge of the bud wood in contact with the edge of the other notch.

What are chip- and T-budding?

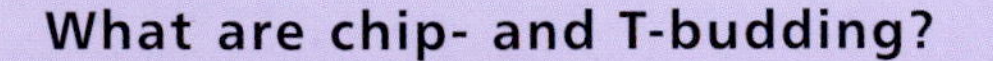

Chip-budding, the technique shown above, is used to propagate woody plants such as *Sorbus*, *Malus* and *Prunus*, on a rootstock grown from seed or hardwood cuttings.

T-budding is often used for summer budding of apples, crab apples, dogwoods and pears. T-budding can only be carried out when the bark is able to 'slip'. This means that, when cut, the bark lifts off easily or peels off without tearing in one uniform layer from the underlying wood.

The exact time when this condition occurs depends on factors such as soil moisture, temperature and the time of year. A T-shaped cut is made and two flaps of bark are opened. The bud is then placed behind the flaps, trimmed off level with the top of the flaps, and secured with tape as for chip-budding.

5 Secure the graft firmly with grafting tape to ensure that the join does not dry out. The graft will usually take about 4–6 weeks in the summer, but winter grafting can take longer.

Landscaping with trees

Garden landscapes are multi-dimensional areas in which we experience the passing seasons and where we can take time out to enjoy the fragrances, colours, sounds, textures and visual stimulation offered by our garden plants, and especially trees.

Trees not only provide height and width, but they also impart a sense of scale. They are so versatile in their many different forms that they can be used in any style of garden. Whether you choose to create a formal or informal scheme, your viewing pleasure will be greatly enhanced by careful landscaping.

Garden trees also enclose areas, mark boundaries, reduce wind and create a microclimate to protect the plants growing beneath them. Carefully selected trees can significantly enhance the beauty of our gardens, which become an extension of our own homes and personalities.

Trees need to fit in with the overall design of a garden. For instance, an oddly placed palm in an English cottage garden will look ill-at-ease, but it can make a stunning focal point when it is sited among complementary plantings. A little pre-planning will help you to avoid costly errors, and this section shows you how.

In this garden surrounded by natural woodland, the trees blend seamlessly with the background, creating a stunning spectacle.

The art of landscaping

Trees are the structural building blocks of any landscape design, and their position and the function you want them to perform should be foremost when planning a garden.

Design principles

Whether you are embarking on a new garden design, or adding trees to an established garden, it is helpful to begin by considering four factors: simplicity, balance, proportion, and rhythm and line.

Simplicity means using the same or similar tree species consistently throughout a design to create cohesion. The planting should follow a straight or slightly curved line, avoiding complex shapes or patterns.

Using symmetry and asymmetry

When you are using trees as part of a cohesive planting scheme, plant either several specimens of similar species or a number of small groups

Attractive walkways can be achieved by fan-training a tree, such as this *Laburnum*, over a framework.

An avenue of trees in a woodland garden can be used to draw the eye into the distance and create a sense of space.

A willow tunnel forms a stunning corridor.

An arrangement of golden and purple-leaved trees can create contrasting background planting.

of the same species so that each group forms a single shape when seen from a distance.

In formal landscapes, trees are often used to provide a symmetrical balance. The trees may form corridors or avenues around an obvious central focal point or around some other axis, with everything on one side being copied on the other, in a mirror-like effect.

Alternatively, asymmetrical design uses different trees on either side of an imaginary axis so that the design has harmony, fluidity and unity along its axis but is not as obviously rigid and balanced as a symmetrical design.

Proportion, rhythm and line

You should ensure that the trees are in scale not only with each other but also with nearby buildings and other structures in the garden. The difficulty lies in the fact that a tree might be in proportion to its surroundings when it is 15–20 years old, but that it might grow too large in either height or breadth as it matures further. For this reason, always consider a tree's ultimate height and spread when you are designing a garden.

Achieving rhythm and line requires the use of more formal landscape techniques. They include the repetitive planting needed in a formal avenue to create a line for the eye to follow into the distance, where a view or focal point, such as a piece of sculpture, can be admired.

Rhythm and line can also be invoked by creating a series of garden rooms using trees and hedges as screens, with the openings framing views into the next room.

Planning a design

The first thing you should do when you are planning a design is to draw a scale plan of your garden.

In order to work out where to position a new tree, you can use triangulation, a technique that fixes the position of an object in relation to the things around it. In order to do this, first find two points already fixed on your plan: the corners of the house are often used. Then go outside and measure the distance from each of the two points to the tree.

Convert these measurements to the scale of the plan, then set a pair of compasses (a compass) to each of the scale distances in turn. For each of the distances, place the point of the compasses on the relevant point on the plan and scribe an arc in the approximate position of the tree. The triangulation point is the spot where the second arc intersects the first.

Landscaping with groups

A group planting of trees should be in harmony with its surroundings. To achieve the best effect the trees should be ranked according to their size, with the smallest ones at the front and the tallest at the back. However, care should be taken to avoid regimentation.

Group plantings

Trees are often evaluated in terms of their ultimate height and spread, and although this can vary according to local growing conditions, it is helpful to define trees in terms of their height:

- Upper-canopy or major shade trees higher than 18m (60ft)
- Upper understorey trees 12–18m (40–60ft) high
- Lower understorey or small garden trees 6–12m (20–40ft) high.

In smaller gardens upper understorey trees will take the place of upper-canopy or major shade trees, and shrubs will take the place of lower understorey trees.

If you are designing a garden from scratch the tree selection process should begin with the larger trees that will form the upper canopy. Work down in scale through the upper understorey and lower understorey, to the lower shrub layers. If you are working within an existing framework, begin by evaluating the trees that are already there, starting with the largest.

It is important that you also consider the relationship of the tree with the plants around it and how the new tree will fit within the wider landscape. For example, if the existing planting includes tropical foliage plants that require lots of sunlight, a dense, broadly spreading tree such as *Acer rubrum* (red maple) would cast too much shade and adversely affect the growth of other plants as it became established. In time it would create so much shade that it would limit the growth of the tropical foliage plants, and its overall appearance would probably be out of keeping with the wider landscape.

A group of *Washingtonia robusta* (thread palm) would be more fitting in this setting. Their bold foliage would provide a strong contrast with other tropical plants and would create less shade than the maple

In a cooler climate *Trachycarpus fortunei* (Chusan palm) would be a hardier option. If a greater level of dappled shade is required, *Jacaranda*

This group of Japanese maples have been carefully selected and positioned. The result is a very attractive group that fits into the surroundings well.

mimosifolia would lightly shade the tropical foliage plants, and its fern-like foliage and attractive flowers would be in perfect harmony with its surroundings. A hardier choice with the same attributes would be *Robinia pseudoacacia* (false acacia).

Gardening in layers

Planting trees in mixed groups increases the amount of diversity in habit, height and spread and foliage and the seasonal variation in flowers, fruit and foliage. It will also help to attract wildlife to the garden in greater numbers and variety. Before deciding on the trees you want to plant, consider the relationships between the different trees and how they will interact.

As a starting point the planting might consist of an upper-canopy tree, a series of upper understorey trees and several different lower understorey trees to create a stepped or layered effect. Planting in this way has other benefits, including creating a microclimate and providing a woodland effect that is attractive to other plants, while also acting as a windbreak.

The upper canopy should consist of trees that are fast-growing and that can tolerate competition for light, nutrients and water. They should be hardy and suitable for your garden.

The upper understorey and lower understorey trees must be shade tolerant and able to compete with the taller, more dominant upper-canopy trees.

To achieve a natural-looking effect do not plant trees in straight lines and remember to space the trees according to their ultimate height and spread. For example, a mature *Acer platanoides* (Norway maple) will grow to an optimum height of 25m (80ft) and spread of 15m (50ft), so a smaller upper understorey tree should not be planted any closer than 7m (23ft) from it trunk.

In general, plant no closer than half the radius of the spread of the tree. In the case of two specimens of *A. platanoides* a distance of 10–15m (33–50ft) would be appropriate and would allow the canopies of the two trees to blend naturally. However, this distance may take a long time to fill in, so additional trees can be planted around the main tree and removed once the main tree is beginning to make an impact. To achieve this, the gardener must be brave and ensure that 'filler' trees or shrubs are removed.

Year-round appeal should be considered when you are planting groups of trees. Here, the birch provides autumn and winter appeal, while the cherry tree is at its stunning best in spring.

Nurse species

A fast-growing tree that is used to protect a slower growing tree is often referred to as a nurse species. It is important that nurse trees are removed once they are no longer needed, otherwise the group planting will become too dense and the overall natural feeling will be lost. Remember, they are only there to provide protection for the more prized trees.

If a quick effect is required the trees can be planted at a much tighter density and will compete more directly against each other, but if you do this then they will require regular pruning to limit their size if all the trees are to continue to occupy their positions.

Landscaping for avenues

An avenue or allée of trees is a double row of trees of the same or similar species, planted in straight lines to create a formal avenue, or curved lines to follow a drive or pathway. They can be planted along the sides of a path or road to form a screen, to frame a vista or to direct the attention to a distant object, such as a statue or feature in the landscape.

Creating symmetry

Allées, avenues and boulevards (another name for a street lined with trees) have always been popular in landscape design because they allow a formal axis to be developed, thereby creating formal symmetry in the garden landscape.

Allées

Originally introduced as a landscape feature during the Renaissance in Italy, allées were widely planted throughout Europe during the seventeenth and eighteenth centuries as a feature in formal landscape gardens. The word allée derives from the French *aller*, meaning 'to go', and refers to a walkway or drive bordered by rows of evenly spaced trees of the same species and of a similar age.

Avenues

Although the grandeur and scale of the avenue planting that took place in the landscaped gardens of the past are difficult to re-create in suburban gardens, avenues are still being planted in our cities. On a smaller scale, a short avenue, created from small, fastigiate trees, can be an interesting linking feature in any garden large enough to accommodate it.

One of the most difficult aspects of planting an avenue is determining the spacing between trees and the spacing between the parallel rows. The trees must be allowed sufficient room for their lower branches to develop, and there must be enough space between the rows to make the avenue usable. If the space between the rows is too wide the avenue may not succeed in its purpose of framing or enhancing a view, and if the trees are too close together the avenue will be overcrowded.

For example, an avenue of *Tilia* x *europaea* (common lime), which has a canopy spread of about 15m (50ft), should be planted 10m (33ft) from a path that is about 2m (6ft) wide so that there is 22m (72ft) between the rows.

However, if a tighter, cathedral avenue is required, the trees could be planted so that there is 18–20m (60–65ft) between the rows, which would eventually lead to the avenue being enclosed by the canopies.

If your garden is large enough to accommodate it, a pollarded avenue can be an interesting feature.

Trees suitable for planting in small avenues

Acer buergerianum (trident maple)
A. campestre cvs.
A. griseum (paperbark maple)
A. palmatum (Japanese maple)
Butia capitata (jelly palm)
Carpinus betulus (common hornbeam)
C. betulus 'Frans Fontaine'
C. caroliniana (American hornbeam)
Cornus florida (flowering dogwood)
C. kousa (kousa dogwood)
C. Stellar hybrids
Cupressus sempervirens Stricta Group
Koelreuteria
Laburnum x *watereri* 'Vossii'
Lagerstroemia spp.
Magnolia spp. and cvs.
Malus spp. and cvs. (crab apple)
Olea europaea (European olive)
Paniculata cvs. (golden raintree)
Pinus sylvestris Fastigiata Group
Robinia x *margaretta* 'Pink Cascade'
R. pseudoacacia 'Frisia' (golden false acacia)
R. x *slavinii* 'Hillieri'
Sorbus spp. (mountain ash)
Stewartia spp.
Trachycarpus fortuneii spp.

Trees suitable for planting in large and medium-sized avenues

Acer platanoides (Norway maple)
A. pseudoplatanus (sycamore)
A. pycnanthum (Japanese red maple)
A. rubrum (red maple)
A. hippocastanum (horse chestnut)
A. indica (Indian horse chestnut)
A. turbinata (Japanese horse chestnut)
Agathis australis (kauri pine)
Araucaria araucana (monkey puzzle)
A. bidwillii (bunya-bunya)
A. cunninghamii (Moreton Bay pine)
Bauhinia spp. (mountain ebony)
Brownea macrophylla (Panama flame tree)
Calocedrus decurrens (incense cedar)
Calophyllum inophyllum (Alexandrian laurel)
Cassia spp. (shower tree)
Castanea sativa (sweet chestnut)
Catalpa bignonioides (Indian bean tree)
Cedrus atlantica Glauca Group
C. deodara (deodar)
Clusia major (autograph tree)
Corylus colurna (Turkish hazel)
Cryptomeria japonica (Japanese cedar)
Cunninghamia lanceolata (Chinese fir)
Davidia involucrata (handkerchief tree)
Dillenia indica (chulta)
Elaeocarpus angustifolius (blue quandong)
Eucalyptus spp. (gum tree)
Fagus grandifolia (American beech)
F. orientalis (oriental beech)
F. sylvatica (common beech)
F. sylvatica 'Dawyck'
Ficus spp. (fig)
Metasequoia glyptostroboides (dawn redwood)
Platanus spp. (plane)
Quercus spp. (oak)
Salix spp. (willow)
Sciadopitys verticillata (Japanese umbrella pine)
Sequoiadendron giganteum 'Glaucum'
Tabebuia spp.
Taxodium distichum (swamp cypress)
Tilia spp. (lime)
Ulmus spp. (elm)
Zelkova spp.

Formal avenues of *Tilia* x *europaea* (common lime) have been used throughout history to create majestic avenues and allées, due to its height and shape.

Planting distances

The planting distances between each individual tree forming the avenue will depend on the type of tree species used, and the following table indicates the recommended distance for the most commonly used species for avenue planting:

Acer platanoides (Norway maple)	10m (33ft)
Aesculus hippocastanum (horse chestnut)	10–15m (33–50ft)
Araucaria araucana (monkey puzzle)	10m (33ft)
Castanea sativa (sweet chestnut)	10–15m (33–50ft)
Cedrus deodara (deodar)	10–15m (33–50ft)
Fagus sylvatica (common beech)	10–15m (33–50ft)
Jacaranda mimosifolia	7–10m (23–33ft)
Platanus x *hispanica* (London plane)	10–15m (33–50ft)
Prunus sargentii (Sargent cherry)	7m (23ft)
Quercus petraea (sessile oak)	10–15m (33–50ft)
Quercus robur (common oak)	10–15m (33–50ft)
Tilia cordata (small-leaved lime)	7–10m (23–33ft)
Tilia x *europaea* (common lime)	7–10m (23–33ft)
Tilia platyphyllos (broad-leaved lime)	7–10m (23–33ft)
Ulmus parvifolia (Chinese elm)	15m (50ft)

Landscaping with garden dividers

Trees can be successfully used as hedges, screens and windbreaks to provide shelter, make garden rooms and create microclimates by slowing wind movement.

Barriers

In order for trees to be effective as barriers, the wind must be able to pass through them rather than being deflected over the top, which has the unwanted effect of creating an area of low pressure behind the barrier. This sucks down the wind to create a turbulent area behind the barrier known as an eddy.

The aim when using trees as a barrier is to slow down the strength of the wind over as long a distance as is practicable before it can return to full strength.

A mixed evergreen and deciduous barrier can provide shelter for a distance of about 20 times the height of the barrier on the downwind side, and about three times its height on the upwind side. The wind will sweep around the ends of the belt as well as over the top, leaving a triangular sheltered zone behind the barrier.

The most effective barriers to the wind are those that contain a mixture of evergreen and deciduous trees, creating 40–50 per cent permeability through the barrier.

Screens and windbreaks

Consisting of narrow bands of trees, sometimes just one tree deep, screens and windbreaks are planted to provide shelter from the wind. Careful planting is required on the windward side so that the air is deflected up and over the taller trees, reducing turbulence on the leeward side.

Windbreaks direct wind over and through or around areas that need to be sheltered. This reduction in wind speed has many benefits in the garden, including improved growth, fewer misshapen trees and shrubs, warmer temperatures in winter and shade in summer.

Narrow belts are effective in most gardens, although wider belts will give considerably more protection if garden space can be sacrificed. The trees are planted in staggered rows or randomly spaced, allowing 2.4m (8ft) between trees and 1.8m (6ft) between rows. Where maximum shelter is required from minimum width, plant tall-growing trees on the windward edge, with smaller trees on the leeward side. Mixed planting of conifers and deciduous material will increase the permeability of the windbreak.

The overall height of the barrier is the most important factor, because this will determine the area behind the windbreak that is protected. For example, a permeable barrier 1.8m (6ft) tall will slow down the wind for up to 20m (65ft) before it picks up to full strength again. The taller the windbreak, the greater the zone of protection, but the less permeable the windbreak the shorter the zone.

Diversity of planting within a shelter-belt or screen can dramatically increase the range of wildlife seen in the garden.

A single row of poplars can be used to form an effective windbreak in the garden.

Hedges

Garden hedges, unlike windbreaks and screens, are usually planted with a single species, most often evergreens, which gives a more formal appearance than a mixed planting, but is a less effective windbreak.

Hedges can be used in many ways in a garden: they create a barrier that encloses the garden and gives privacy and protection from intruders; they provide a boundary to the garden to divide the property from its neighbours; they protect plants within the garden from the elements by creating a microclimate; they obscure unwanted views and eyesores; and they can be used within a garden to create separate 'rooms'.

Depending on the species chosen, hedges can be left to grow and trimmed annually so they are informal or clipped regularly to create neat, formal boundaries.

Hedges grown from trees are normally planted in a double staggered row, with rows positioned about 1.8m (6ft) apart and the trees in each row also about 1.8m (6ft) apart. While the plants are establishing it is important to keep the base weed-free so that the hedge is fully furnished down to soil level.

Hedges are generally clipped to produce a flat-topped or rounded hedge with sloping sides. Hedges should be wider at the base so that snow slides off. Formal hedges may require one or two trims a year depending on the species, and evergreen hedges generally require more clipping than deciduous ones.

Deciduous trees such as beech and hornbeams make very attractive hedges that will exhibit more seasonal variation than the more traditional evergreen screen.

Pleached hedges

Often called 'hedges on stilts' or 'aerial hedges', pleached hedges comprise trees that have been trained to form a hedge while leaving clear and visible trunks. The word pleaching is derived from the French word *plessier*, which means to intertwine or knot, and it has been practised since the Middle Ages.

Pleached hedges can be used to create boundaries in the garden, and in some situations a pleached hedge looks more attractive than a hedge that is furnished down to the ground. They are often planted in double rows to form an avenue, when the branches at the top are trained to create a tunnel, and they can also frame views and walkways.

Pleaching a hedge takes several years. Begin by planting a row of flat-headed trees at equal intervals against a framework of posts that are at least 3m (10ft) tall and to which parallel wires are attached along its length, about 30cm (12in) apart, with the first wire 1–1.2m (3–4ft) from the ground. The young lateral branches are trained along the wires, while sideways growth is allowed to develop to the required depth of the hedge, which is usually less than 1m (3ft).

The hedge section is clipped annually to produce the required hedge effect, and branches on the trunks are gradually cleared to the desired height to create the stilts effect. Lime trees, such as *Tilia cordata* (small-leaved lime) and *T.* x *platyphyllos* (broad-leaved lime), are most often planted for this purpose, although *Ulmus* spp. (elm), *Fraxinus* spp. (ash) and *Carpinus* spp. hornbeam) can also used.

Trees suitable for use as hedges or windbreaks

Abies spp. (silver fir)
Acer campestre (field maple)
Alnus cordata (Italian alder)
Araucaria araucana (monkey puzzle)
Banksia spp.
Bauhinia spp. (mountain ebony)
Calliandra spp. (powder puff tree)
Callistemon spp. (bottlebrush)
Calocedrus decurrens (incense cedar)
Calodendron capense (Cape chestnut)
Calophyllum inophyllum (Alexandrian laurel)
Carpinus betulus (common hornbeam)
C. betulus 'Frans Fontaine'
C. caroliniana (American hornbeam)
Chamaecyparis lawsoniana (Lawson cypress)
Clusia major (autograph tree)
Crataegus spp. (hawthorn)
Cryptomeria japonica (Japanese cedar
x *Cupressocyparis leylandii* (Leyland cypress)
Dillenia indica (chulta)
Elaeocarpus angustifolius (blue quandong)
Eucalyptus spp. (gum tree)
Fagus sylvatica (common beech)
Ficus spp. (fig)
Grevillea spp. (spider flower)
Pinus sylvestris Fastigiata Group
Populus spp. (poplar)
Sorbus spp. (mountain ash)
Thuja koraiensis (Korean arborvitae)
Taxus baccata (yew)
Thujopsis dolobrata (hiba)
Tilia spp. (lime)
Tsuga canadensis (eastern hemlock)
T. heterophylla (western hemlock)

Trees as focal points or backdrops

Selecting a tree for a focal point in the lawn or as a specimen elsewhere in the garden is one of the most difficult choices because the tree must be in scale with the overall garden but also attractive enough to provide interest. Choosing a tree for such a position is as subjective as selecting a piece of sculpture for a prominent place in the garden.

Trees as focal points

A tree that is going to be used as a lawn specimen or a focal point needs to be as attractive as possible throughout the year, so ideally it should have at least one of the following attributes:

- Eye-catching habit or shape, such as columnar, conical, pyramidal or weeping (see pages 34–41)
- Attractive foliage, whether deciduous or evergreen, coloured in summer (yellow, purple, blue or variegated) or boldly architectural, such as a palm or the leaves of *Catalpa bignonioides* (Indian bean tree)
- Beautiful flowers, such as a spring-flowering cherry or summer-flowering jacaranda
- Colourful fruits, such as the yellow-orange fruits of *Eriobotrya japonica* (loquat) or the ivory-white berries of *Sorbus cashmeriana* (Kashmir rowan)
- Attractive bark, especially if it flakes like that of *Acer griseum* (paperbark maple) or *Pinus bungeana* (lacebark pine)
- Attractive twigs, which are less obvious in the growing season but can be appreciated in winter; maples are noted for their attractive twigs, including the scarlet ones of *Acer palmatum* 'Sango-kaku' (coral bark maple) or the salmon-pink, orange and yellow branches of *Acer* x *conspicuum* 'Phoenix'.

Scale and position

A lawn tree should look like an extension of the surrounding tree and shrub layers or as if a clearing has been cut through a wooded area.

The most important factors when planting a focal point tree are the size of the tree and the distance from it to the nearest trees or shrubs. It is important to allow enough space for the tree to look comfortable in its landscape.

This distance should be at least half to three-quarters of the height of the tree when it is fully mature, measured from the outer point of the nearest tree canopy to the trunk of the proposed specimen.

It can be helpful to hammer a tree stake into the ground where the proposed tree is to be planted and walk around the garden and house to view it from different locations, moving the stake about until you locate the right spot.

Determining the position of a focal point can be done by viewing the garden from various windows – the kitchen or sitting room, for example – or by identifying a view or part of the garden to which you want to direct the viewer.

Trees as backdrops

A mixed border planting in a small garden performs the same role as a wooded area in a larger garden, and when they are used in this way trees provide shade and protection for the shrubs and herbaceous material beneath them. Trees in borders have a number of functions, including providing a foil or backdrop for the border plants that surround them and providing an additional seasonal interest with their architectural form.

Trees that are grown to provide a backdrop for border plants should have relatively plain foliage that is a uniform colour. Most evergreen

Magnolia stellata is a stunning tree that produces star-shaped white flowers and which makes a fantastic focal point specimen in the garden.

Lawn specimen and focal point trees

Acer griseum (paperbark maple)
A. negundo 'Flamingo'
A. palmatum (Japanese maple)
A. pensylvanicum (striped maple)
A. pseudoplatanus 'Brilliantissimum'
Araucaria araucana (monkey puzzle)
Betula albosinensis var. *septentrionalis*
B. ermanii (Erman's birch)
B. utilis var. *jacquemontii* (Himalayan birch)
Bismarckia nobilis (noble palm)
Butia capitata (pindo palm)
Calliandra spp. (powder puff tree)
Calocedrus decurrens (incense cedar)
Cassia spp. (shower tree)
Castanea sativa 'Albomarginata'
Catalpa bignonioides 'Aurea'
Cercidiphyllum japonicum f. *pendulum*
Cornus kousa
Cupressus sempervirens Stricta Group
Dillenia indica (chulta)
Elaeocarpus angustifolius (blue quandong)
Eucalyptus spp. (gum tree)
Fraxinus excelsior 'Pendula' (weeping ash)
Gleditsia triacanthos 'Sunburst'
Jacaranda mimosifolia
Koelreuteria paniculata 'Fastigiata'
Lagerstroemia spp.
Livistona spp. (fountain palm)
Magnolia spp. and cvs.
Malus spp. and cvs. (crab apple)
Melia azedarach 'Jade Snowflake'
Metasequoia glyptostroboides 'Gold Rush'
Olea europaea (European olive)
Phoenix spp. (date palm)
Robinia pseudoacacia 'Frisia'
Roystonea spp. (royal palm)
Sciadopitys verticillata (Japanese umbrella pine)
Stewartia spp.
Tabebuia spp.
Taxodium distichum var. *imbricatum* 'Nutans'
Tilia tomentosa 'Petiolaris'
Trachycarpus spp.
Washingtonia spp.

trees fit these criteria, and their deep or light green foliage is an excellent background for flowering shrubs and herbaceous plants.

Trees that are used to enhance a mixed border should follow the same selection process as trees for focal points. However, the selection of both must also consider the scale of the planting so that the tree doesn't dominate the border. A tree for a mixed border should be at least three times the overall depth of the border. For example, a border 3m (10ft) deep could accommodate a tree about 9m (30ft) tall, depending on its spread and form.

Any tree selection for such a location should provide light dappled shade so that sufficient light can penetrate the canopy.

Embothrium coccineum (Chilean fire bush) makes a spectacular lawn specimen.

The purple foliage of this focal point tree not only gives height and structure to the border, but also provides a contrasting colour for the surrounding herbaceous planting.

Landscaping for woodland

Using trees to create areas of woodland in the garden offers considerable potential for planting a wide range of species that would naturally grow in shady to semi-shaded locations.

Creating a woodland area

Woodland in a garden should be a scaled-down version of natural woodland and as such should create habitats that include deep shade, dappled shade and sunny woodland edge or fringe planting. So that sufficient light can still enter the garden, lower limbs can be removed from the trees to allow shrubs and herbaceous plants to develop beneath and around them.

The most important decision facing the gardener who wants to create a woodland area is whether to use native or exotic trees to create the upper canopy. A woodland planted with native species will create and support higher levels of biodiversity than one composed entirely of exotic species, although its aesthetic value may not be as great. A mixture of both, however, can provide a balance, both being aesthetically pleasing and having the potential to support biodiversity.

Whichever decision is made, the trees chosen should include both deciduous and evergreen species to provide year-round cover for wildlife; trees and shrubs that flower throughout the year (early and late flowers are especially important for bees); and fruit- or berry-bearing trees and shrubs to provide food for native and migratory animals.

Woodland areas in gardens are an invaluable source of food and shelter for a wide range of native and migratory animals. Here, a red squirrel buries an acorn in a sunny patch of the woodland floor.

Many wild flowers, such as daffodils, bluebells, primroses and foxgloves, grow naturally in woodland areas, and provide a stunning display of spring colour in your garden.

Tree densities can vary, but ideally species should be planted at distances that are equal to half their ultimate spread when they are mature. For example, a tree that will eventually has a spread of 10m (33ft) should be planted at a distance of no less than 5m (16ft) from the centre of the neighbouring tree.

Varying the planting distance will help to create a range of habitats, which can most easily be achieved by planting a small grove of trees with different canopy heights or creating areas of coppice or shrub. A more open wooded area will attract a greater diversity of wildlife, although such openness can allow in the elements, making it less suitable for some types of less robust plant.

The same rules apply to planting a group of trees for a woodland as for planting a shelter-belt or windbreak (see page 148).

Dead and decaying wood piles can provide habitats for small mammals, insects and fungi. As the wood slowly decays, nutrients are released into the soil, which in turn benefit the trees.

To provide maximum wind protection the planting should contain a mixture of deciduous and evergreen trees to provide permeability, which slows down, rather than deflecting, the wind. Denser shrub planting around the edge of the woodland area will offer cover for wildlife and at the same time protect the inner woodland areas from potential wind damage.

Managing woodland gardens

Woodland areas require attention to ensure that enough light enters the area for the trees to flourish, creating dappled shade. The lower branches of upper-canopy trees should be removed in order to allow lower-canopy trees to survive, a process that should be carried out regularly as part of an annual cycle when the lowest whorl of branches is removed. In the short term, nurse trees (see page 145) can be used for shelter while the upper-canopy trees are allowed to mature.

A newly planted woodland garden will need thinning and pruning to prevent the under-storey planting becoming congested and create a good diversity of habitats.

You can coppice some of the trees if you like (see pages 118–19), and if you do not need to use the resultant cut wood, it can be left in piles to rot, which will help to increase biodiversity.

Woodland clearings appear naturally when individual trees die and fall, but you may need to thin the trees further to ensure that enough light penetrates the upper canopy and reaches the woodland floor, in order to encourage a wide range of plants.

Landscaping with conifers

There is a very wide range of conifers available for planting in the garden. These vary in size, shape, colour and form, but all of them can be used to provide the structural backbone of planting schemes.

Versatile conifers

Although most commonly planted to create windbreaks, conifers can also be used for structural planting, to create traditional or unusual looking avenues, as focal points in lawns or mixed borders, and as upper- and lower-canopy trees, where they will display year-round interest, striking silhouettes and in some cases spectacular autumn colour.

The word conifer means 'cone-bearer' and this indicates that the seeds of these trees are protected in a cone or a cone-like structure. There are many different evergreen trees that make up the conifer group, including cypress, cedar, fir, juniper, larch, pine and spruce, as well as western red cedar or thuja, which is normally grown for hedging.

However, there is also a smaller group of conifers that lose their needles-like leaves in autumn. These include the larch, dawn redwood, and the swamp and pond cypress, and it is these varieties that produce the most spectacular autumn hues.

Conifers provide year-round interest, but come into their own during the winter months when they add a splash of colour to a winter garden.

Conifers are highly adaptable trees and their size can range from gigantic, like the Giant Redwood (*Sequoiadendron giganteum*), to a small pin-cushion-sized conifer, such as the Norway spruce (*Picea abies* 'Nana Compacta'), which will grow to just 30cm (12in). In their native habitats, where deciduous trees would fail, conifers may face freezing temperatures, driving winds, swamp-like soils and baking sun. This means that they will tolerate almost any conditions, making them extremely useful garden trees.

Many conifers have distinctive shapes, unusual habits, attractive bark and amazing cones. Their needles range in colour from hues of bronze and gold to blue and green, and some even display variegated needles with gold and green or green and white.

With such a diverse array of conifers to choose from, there is certain to be a species suitable for every location in the garden.

Using conifers

The use of conifers as garden trees is forever going in and out of vogue with gardeners, even though they possess the desirable qualities of providing year-round interest and being relatively maintenance-free.

Conifers were traditionally planted to accompany heaths in heather gardens, used with alpine plants and other dwarf shrubs in rock gardens, or even planted on their own in more specialized botanical collections like pinetums, where their different shapes and forms are shown to their full extent. However, conifers do not need to be restricted to such specialized companion planting, and they can easily be incorporated in more traditional garden settings.

Dwarf conifers

As a result of the growing number of smaller-sized gardens, there is an increasing demand for smaller trees, which has in turn led to an interest dwarf conifers.

Although the definition of what constitutes a 'dwarf' tree varies, they are generally trees that grow to a maximum height of 1.8m (5.9ft) over ten years. There are many dwarf varieties available, including *Chamaecyparis lawsoniana* 'Gnome', *Juniperus communis* 'Compressa' and *Picea abies* 'Little Gem', and they make useful, attractive specimens when they are grown in containers or rockeries.

Dwarf conifers are easy to grow since they naturally maintain neat shapes, so very little pruning or trimming is required. Although they are highly adaptable and will tolerate a wide range of habitats, they will not tolerate competition from more vigorous garden varieties and are easily shaded out by larger conifers, which can quickly and easily outgrow their alloted space.

Conifers in avenues

The different shapes of conifers can provide a distinct outline when they are used in avenues. In traditional situations monkey puzzle (*Araucaria araucana*), deodar cedar (*Cedrus deodara*), larch (*Larix decidua*) or Scots pine (*Pinus sylvestris*) have all been used to great effect.

However, the weeping habit of Nootka cypress (*Chamaecyparis nootkatensis*) or Brewer's spruce (*Picea breweriana*) can be used to introduce a graceful and more unusual look. If space is at a premium then you can create a Mediterranean look by planting an avenue of Italian cypress (*Cupressus sempervirens*) or Chinese juniper (*Juniperus chinensis* 'Aurea').

Conifers develop a range of habits, including upright, conical and spreading. Planted together in the garden they can make a striking group.

Conifers as focal points

As a result of their unique and distinctive shapes, conifers make ideal focal point trees. The use of a deciduous conifer – such as *Metasequoia glyptostrboides* 'Gold Rush', which has striking yellow foliage that turns a pinkish brown in autumn, as well as a distinctive outline and fluted brown bark – as a winter feature in such a location can add a dramatic element to a garden.

Conifers in borders

The bright foliage and interesting shapes of many conifers make them suitable for any border, as long as they do not get shaded out by other plants. Tall, narrow species, such as *Taxus baccata* 'Fastigiata Aureomarginata', are ideal for adding height to a shrub border, while spherical ones, such as *Thuja occidentalis* 'Danica', add shape to a border of dainty perennials.

Landscaping with palms

Except in tropical garden landscapes, palms remain one of the most underused landscape trees. This is probably due to the fact that their form and foliage create a very tropical look, which can appear out of place in gardens in temperate regions.

Using palm trees

Although palms are often difficult to site in temperate landscapes, it is worth persevering as not only do they have bold linear trunks and exotic foliage, but these plants also provide an air of tropical lushness in any garden situation.

Palms can be used in a variety of ways in the landscape. They can provide the shade and upper-canopy produced by a major shade tree; they can be used to create formal avenues; they make excellent lawn specimens and focal points; and they can be used in tropical foliage borders.

Palm trees can thrive in a variety of different habitats, including tropical rainforests, exposed, salt-laden beaches, mangrove swamps, oases of deserts, tropical and temperate mixed forests – and a few species are able to survive occasional freezing temperatures in temperate regions of the world.

An abundance of palms creates a luxurious, tropical effect as well as providing shade and protection for other plants and wildlife.

In fact, a surprising number of temperate gardens can successfully incorporate palms into the design, and they can establish and grow quite quickly if they are provided with the optimum growing conditions.

Nevertheless, the fact remains that the largest distribution and greatest diversity of palm trees are found throughout tropical zones of the world, and this stunning array provides us with a massive selection of highly desirable landscape trees that are grown for their attractive architectural form, fern-like foliage, distinctive and slender hessian-covered trunks, attractive flowers and interesting, sometimes edible, fruits.

In tropical climates palms are easier to accommodate and can be used to great effect as the dominant tree in the landscape. Careful selection and combining of the palms in the landscape can produce a wide variety of foliage shapes, colour, texture and heights, while providing an evergreen backdrop to show other plants against.

Palms for temperate areas

Although many gardens will simply be too cold for palms, there are some varieties that are hardier than most people realize, and it is worth growing these if you can – their wonderful habit and foliage will introduce an air of tropical lushness to even the dreariest of temperate gardens.

Just like any other landscape tree, palms make ideal focal point plants in the garden, with their bold foliage that can be either feathery, fern-like (pinnate) or fan-shaped (palmate), and their linear growing habit, which provides one of the most distinct silhouettes in the landscape.

Palms are often planted as lawn specimens, either singly or in small groups, with the close-cut lawn

In temperate climates, palms and cordylines create stunning landscapes if they are planted with care and thought.

adding to the formality of the arrangement. When positioned as if a piece of sculpture, a specimen palm can be viewed from all sides, dominating the landscape with its bold, architectural foliage and trunk.

Although palm trees can be used as a single specimen, they are best planted in groups, as this style of planting seems more natural, provides more of a focal point and helps to harmonize them with their surroundings. Planting in groups also provides shade and protection for the plants that can flourish below them.

Whether grown singly or in loose groups, one major benefit of palm trees is they do not cast dense shade unless they are planted very tightly together. Many palms have adapted to become highly shade tolerant and as such make excellent lower-canopy trees, with larger trees above, and providing an attractive feature that casts little shade below.

In many tropical countries, palms are grown in formal avenues or along the sides of roads, where their linear form creates a strong formality with the symmetry of the roadside verges; their stems remain cleanly exposed as any dying leaves can be removed to show off their attractive stems.

Palm trees are very adaptable and are able to survive in soils that are low in nutrients, and in areas with only occasional rainfall. As they are tolerant of salt spray and scorching winds, many palms are found in coastal locations. However, the one thing they do dislike is very compacted soils.

For temperate regions, specialized microclimates are required and only the most hardy of cold-resistant palms will grow.

Palms for tropical and temperate climates

For tropical, subtropical and Mediterranean regions:
Bismarckia nobilis (noble palm)
Caryota mitis (fishtail palm)
Licuala grandis (ruffled fan palm)
Livistonia australis (cabbage palm)
Roystonea regia (regal palm)
Washingtonia filifera (thread palm)

For temperate regions:
Butia capitata (jelly palm)
Chamaerops humilis (fan palm)
Phoenix canariensis (date palm)
Trachycarpus fortunei (Chusan palm)

Index

Magnolia grandiflora 'Goliath'

Taxus baccata

Magnolia campbellii